Against the Grain

Against the Grain

Coming Through Mid-life Crisis

David J. Maitland

The Pilgrim Press
New York

The poem on p. 42 is "A Puzzlement" from *The King and I*. Copyright © 1951 by Richard Rodgers & Oscar Hammerstein. Copyright renewed, Williamson Music, Inc., owner of publication and allied rights throughout the Western Hemisphere and Japan. International copyright secured. All rights reserved. Used by permission. The poem on pp. 136-37 is "Saint Francis and the Sow" from *Mortal Acts, Mortal Words* by Galway Kinnell. Copyright © 1980 by Galway Kinnell. Reprinted by permission of Houghton Mifflin Company. Biblical quotations are from the Revised Standard Version of the Bible, copyright 1946, 1952, and © 1971 by the Division of Christian Education, National Council of Churches, and are used by permission.

Library of Congress Cataloging in Publication Data

Maitland, David Johnston, 1922-
  Against the grain.

  Includes bibliographical references.
1. Middle age—Religious life.
2. Middle age—Psychological aspects.
3. Maitland, David Johnston, 1922-
I. Title.   BV4579.5.M34   248.8'4   81-10595
ISBN 0-8298-0461-7   AACR2
ISBN 0-8298-0675-X (pbk.)

The Pilgrim Press, 132 West 31 Street, New York, New York 10001

To Betsy, Todd and Jim

for endless stimulation and responsiveness
but, especially, for patience and generosity of spirit

Contents

To the Reader

Since this book is the result of reflections on my own experience, I have wondered about the audience for whom it was written. By my own experience I mean at least the following: my family and place of origin; a lot of formal education, especially theological (my mother wondered if I wasn't overdoing it!); thirty-five years of marriage and parenthood; a quarter century as Chaplain and teacher of religion at an academically intense college in the mid-west; an abiding concern for an intelligent understanding of Christian faith and for the ramifications of that faith in personal and societal life; and, in the course of coming to grips with the dislocations of my own middle years, a profound influence by some social science theories of human development. These experiences, plus a good deal neither here suggested nor yet recognized, underlie this book. While I do not assume that anyone shares my precise concerns or perspective, I trust that much of what I have written will be recognizable from the reader's own experience.

With this in mind I can now say I have written for those for whom at least some of the following things are true: they have begun to recognize as illusions—which is not a negative term—some of the commitments and convictions which moved them beyond adolescence; they wonder about the tasks and satisfactions which may lie in what Jung calls "life's afternoon;" having lived purposefully to date and with mixed pleasure, they are not disposed to trivialize or to mark time for the balance of their days; they maintain some hope, often tenuous and seemingly without warrant, that there is an understanding of

Christian faith relevant to the uncertainty of mid-life. The audience thus is educated, vaguely aware of some unanticipated malaise which they are reluctant to acknowledge and unable to discuss, oversold on some of the illusions of American society, willing to search for some better understanding of the conditions of human fulfillment, still looking for a form of faith relevant to the ills of both society and self. The reader so equipped should not find my observations utterly idiosyncratic. S/he—which is how I shall handle those pronouns—should recognize in his/her life analogous experience. That we agree throughout in our interpretations of similar episodes is neither likely nor desirable.

Those with little religious interest may wish to concentrate on chapters 2-7. Chapter 2, "Looking Both Ways," and chapter 7, "In Praise of Aging," concentrate on problems and abilities which are heightened during the middle years. Sandwiched between this backward- and forward-looking material are four chapters on the two primary relationships of life: work, by which our abilities and needs are related to the resources and needs of the world; marriage and friendship, in which lies the potential for our deepest humanization. Little that is explicitly religious will be found here other than for reasons intrinsic to a given discussion. Those with religious interests may, however, wish to begin with the first chapter in which I indicate why the stages of human development are germane to maturation in faith. In addition, I have tried to indicate in the concluding chapters a fresh way of viewing the endless dialectic of faith and culture.

It is impossible to acknowledge all those who have helped me formulate the ideas presented in this book. I kept no record of conversations and other encouragements that forced me to take the experiences of my own mid-life seriously. I am indebted to more friends that I can remember, much less name. But, because of the final pressures to complete the manuscript, I am especially aware of the patience and skill of Joan Rietz who found time and energy, where neither existed, to prepare this manuscript.

Also at Carleton College sincere thanks are in order to at least the following people and offices: the Trustees, who granted the sabbatical in which a first draft was completed; the President and the Dean, both for funds to cover some local costs and for encouragement; colleagues in the Department of Religion, especially the Chair, who allowed me to offer a seminar in which some of the issues were explored; and the Secretary for Alumni Affairs, for the opportunities to share some of my reflections with responsive graduates around the country.

Several local churches in Minnesota, especially the congregations at Austin, Owatonna and Northfield, were the first to invite me to share my observations on the importance of the experience of the middle years. For this encouragement I am grateful. And the timing for the first faculty manuscript contest sponsored by the Council on Higher Education of the United Church of Christ was perfect. By selecting my entry the Council provided a singular reassurance. The searching opinions which I began to voice a decade ago, though still incomplete, they judged to be not completely unsound! That was less clear several years ago when I put together a five-part series of sermons and lectures entitled "Faith for Growth" for a radio station at a neighboring college. It was that invitation, however, which enabled me to move my material from scrambled notes to an initial manuscript.

Over the years I have been sustained by many friends but they are in no way responsible for the views voiced here. It was Mark who first listened. I have also benefited from the counsel and concern of Ralph and Mary Helen, Carol, John and Betty, Daniel and Nell, Corky, Elizabeth and John, Ann, Jean, Jim and Wilys Claire. Without their varied encouragements I doubt I would have completed this work.

And finally, long before we could imagine such a thing as mid-life and, fortunately, since that has been left somewhat behind us, Betsy has been the dear person in my life. For more than I shall ever be able to express I am grateful and indebted to her; for things that I may have said here that she would have preferred to have kept between us I apologize. From her and from Todd and Jim I have learned more than I deserved. In that lies love's tutelage. My gratitude verges on idolatry.

In conclusion I would like to add the following: several years ago, after a conversation in which I tried without great success to explain some of the imponderables of my life, Todd wrote something which I have since kept on my desk. People, she said, who keep orderly minds do so by refusing to think of hard things. As may become apparent to the reader I have often found this consoling!

Against the Grain

CHAPTER 1

Paying Attention: Insights from a Sculpture Park

I am convinced of the profound importance of the stages of life through which people ordinarily pass. In this movement from birth to death lie endless opportunities for maturation which I believe are God-given. Sacraments and celebrations have long recognized the significance of certain universal milestones. In addition to these, however, I shall try to show the religious significance of the unheralded, often unnoticed, day-to-day issues with which men and women struggle.

This assertion will be problematical for some readers. For example, if I am understood to be suggesting that the process of life is an irreversible series of boxes, they may insist that this has not been their experience. And they would be right. The language of stages, and the physical changes which accompany them, is misleading to the extent that it implies one-way movement only. We might better think of periods in which a particular configuration of issues prevails. All of life's issues are probably involved at all of the stages but certain of them predominate at different times. For example, the fact of mortality, which may be central as one ages or is in the midst of acute illness, is a minor component in the adolescent's search for identity. It is, however, an ingredient of that configuration just as the adolescent's hard won self-understanding is relevant to later commitments to work or relationships. Many times, though never in quite the same way, we work through the basic issues of our lives. There is a dynamic to this process which the language of stages must not obscure.

Others may be troubled by the universality implied in the assertion that the work of life's stages is God-given. Whether or not the content of these stages, as described by contemporary social scientists, is the same in all societies, or is even the same for men and women in our own, is unclear. Sufficient evidence has not been accumulated. Yet I doubt that present, Western understanding of the progress of lives fully describes human experience. In fact, there is reason to hope that it does not. Other societies may well be wiser in their attitudes toward one or more of the stages, such as aging, than we will ever be, given our present resources.

That our understanding of human development may not be universal stopped bothering me when I realized that the God-givenness does not lie in the particular behavior which we encourage at the various stages. Actions will always vary between societies as they have in different periods for any single group. Our long latency between puberty and full adulthood—almost two decades for some of the professions—requires inner resources which were not needed by the boy who took the plow directly from his father. Likewise, the liberation of women in the last century requires developments which we are only beginning to understand. Time and place will determine somewhat different patterns of maturation. Therefore, the God-givenness of the developmental process is not located simply in contemporary descriptions of what is normal.

We cannot, however, be indifferent to such descriptions. To be viable they must not contradict universal biological developments. A child should no more be held responsible for a perspective which only experience will yield than an elderly person should be expected to have the physical resiliency of the child. There are immutable biological developments in the organism between infancy and age, but they are only part of the human story. Growth always combines biological necessity and social values, and it is from the latter that definitions of what is normal come. There is always some God-givenness in these social expectations. There will also always be demonic ingredients. We must be able to resist "normative" exhortations which will result in sexist, ageist or racist behaviour. As such attitudes go unchallenged, potential maturation is skewed or arrested.

Critical attention must always be paid to societal expectations. This is especially true for expectations which seem to be taken for granted. General agreement about such matters easily leads to the assumption that they are God-given. That this may not be the case is my contention.

The God-givenness of the human potential for maturation lies not in the specific behavior expected at any of life's stages. Rather, it is present in the desire for wholeness. This may sound both innocuous and imprecise; it is neither. An appeal for wholeness constitutes a challenge to prevailing societal expectations. Underlying the desire for wholeness is the realization that there is unacknowledged, or at least underdeveloped, potential yet to be integrated into one's self. Maturation remains incomplete to the extent that there are aspects of my life with which I and others are unfamiliar. While some concealment is probably inevitable, one's potential for good is truncated by unfamiliarity with one's self. Self-knowledge and accurate self-representation, however difficult and incomplete, are always preferable to ignorance and deception.

Greater self-awareness seems harmless as long as we assume that we are only seeking more of the same. The challenge becomes radical once it is recognized that there are anomalous ingredients in the ignored self which seek to be included in the wholeness of a life. It is internal ambivalence, even contradiction, which seeks inclusion. The acknowledgment that this is the nature of our God-givenness sharply contradicts our societal penchant for consistency. It will also be an unfamiliar emphasis in many religious contexts. Every simplification, from which all societies derive their distinctive vitality, is achieved by compromising our God-given desire for wholeness. Inasmuch as all societies attach greater importance to some aspects of the human potential than to others, and inasmuch as we are largely shaped by one society, we tend to prefer our particular simplification. The religious task is to recognize this to be a human condition and to label it properly. The penchant for simplification, for avoiding the God-given capacity for whole-ness, is Sin. That the work of Christian faith is to identify every simplification as only the relative good it is suggests how much misguidance there is in culture-endorsing religion. The rela-tionship of faith to culture is much more dialectical than we are often led to believe. At stake always is the God-givenness of lives which is imperilled by tendencies, both external and internal, to pay attention only to aspects of that wholeness. It is to those parts of our lives that do not conform to societal norms—for instance the need for solitude as well as gregariousness, the inclusion of time for appreciation as well as for usefulness—that we must learn to attend. This concern for wholeness, which is constantly being undermined, is a largely neglected aspect of Christian faith.

As we shall see in greater detail later, this understanding of the desire for wholeness is a concern found in the writings of contemporary theorists of human development. For example, in Erik Erikson's description of a normal human life, in addition to recognizing movement backward and forward in the stages, he emphasizes that there are at each stage tensions which must be resolved without being destroyed. Normal maturation is not a matter of irreversible progress from immaturity to maturity. There is endless backing and filling, repeated modifications of every life-stage, as new demands and hitherto ignored inner resources are recognized. Among such resources are the qualities and attitudes which could not have been employed at an earlier time.

It is for this reason that we must resolve conflicts inherent in a stage of life without assuming that any particular resolution will be final. Many such resolutions are quite adequate at the time; most are less adequate than we pretend; all eventually prove inadequate. Not only is there nothing wrong with this; it is unavoidable. Life moves on. Every resolution is an approxima-tion of what is ideally possible. We do the best we can with what is accessible at any given time. As time passes we are often put in touch with inner resources which were ignored in achieving the original resolution. We didn't see then how they might be incorporated.

Let me briefly illustrate in terms of the Identity Crisis for which Erikson is best known. The tension at this stage of one's life is between the post-puberty need for a viable sense of who one is, on the one hand, and the danger of inadequate self-knowledge and unconvincing self-presentation, on the other. The viability of one's adolescent identity is based upon one's own, and others', ability to recognize threads of continuity between what one has been as a child and what one hopes to become as an adult. Emphasizing this sense of continuity forces one to conceal the inner aspects which, for the time being, don't fit. When these negative aspects predominate we then have the disorder which Erikson calls Identity Diffusion. Clearly some diffusion is inherent in every viable identity. This is not fatal; it only represents past elements and future potential that cannot be integrated at this time! What is dangerous is the need to pretend that there is nothing more than what meets the eye. The more successful this pretension the more difficult it is to evoke the suppressed elements of one's God-given wholeness. We do not need to know at any particular time what to make of all the ingredients of our potential wholeness. All we need is the freedom to acknowledge that there is more to us than either we or others can yet see. It sounds so simple. But for reasons rooted both in societal aversion to ambiguity and personal fear of God-given freedom it is the most demanding assignment.

It is, I believe, this task which faith in God engages. The work of such faith is always twofold: to enable one to see aspects of one's self which it would seem convenient to ignore, and to encourage one to refuse oversimplifications. More accurately, since we cannot both belong to and be wholly at odds with our society, the believer finds him or herself always engaged in a kind of lover's quarrel with the surrounding world. It was something about such quarrels which I began to see on a cold afternoon in Norway about twenty years ago. That hour in Oslo's Frogner Park was especially significant for me because of the sensibilities which I brought to it. At another time the impact might have been quite different.

I was not then, and may never become, a highly introspective person. The fact that my parents were immigrants never caused me to feel alienated from their new land. From my earliest days I realized that my mother used the word home in two ways. Depending chiefly on her mood she referred either to our house or to the place and people from which she had come. While I sensed the depth of her Scots' attachments, I knew them only as kindly relatives who sent Christmas and birthday presents. A basically happy and endlessly hard-working person, she never was able to transfer all emotion from her family of origin to the family which she had created. It was an extraterritorial, extended family into which I had been born.

Whereas my parents' lives were largely confined to associations with fellow Scots, my sense of identity came increasingly from the milieu of a small city in Massachusetts. Football, for example, was not the game that my father knew by the same name. In retrospect I am grateful for the fact that, without abandoning their own roots, they supported almost without murmur my "Americanization." At only one point did they balk: at age eighteen I proposed to borrow several hundred dollars in order to go to college. While they had little enthusiasm for the education I desired—at a much later degree ceremony my mother asked, with mixed pride and skepticism, "David, lad, do you ever wonder if you could be getting educated beyond your intelligence?"—it was the borrowing of money which they could not abide. Beyond their ability to imagine how such a loan would be repaid, they simply did not believe that good could come from it. By signing the loan I took a final step toward a way of life which had long been taking shape. About this decision I had no uncertainty. Though my cousins might apprentice themselves to their parents' trades, formal education was to be the means by which I would realize the dream that had eluded my parents. Without much personal reflection I poured myself into the basically satisfying tasks of work and family for the next two decades. While neither was problem-free, I would not have had it otherwise. There was always much "out there" to do and it all furthered the acculturation on which I had embarked. There was no going back.

To what extent these factors of personal history contributed to my mid-life malaise I do not know. What is clear is that my conscious introspection began quite unexpectedly. I was looking at some sculpture when it happened.

Perhaps it was just a fortunate coincidence that I was then forty years old. In all events, my encounter with the work of Gustav Vigeland in Frogner Park began an important process within me: to learn to take more seriously the various stages of human life, especially the stage at which I found myself. Eventually I came to see that *God calls us to faith by calling us to ourselves wherever we are in the life cycle.* While the Word of God remains constant the words that an adolescent can hear are quite different from those to which a grandparent may be attuned. What I experienced amidst outdoor sculpture in a foreign city might well not have occurred a decade earlier or later in my life.

Let me take you to Oslo. In about two hundred pieces of sculpture distributed over a large city park Gustav Vigeland tells the human story from cradle to grave. From happy and frightened children, to shy but interested adolescents, to mutually attracted but equally withdrawn young adults, to loving but sometimes cruel parents, to lonely but sometimes cared-for aged, Vigeland depicts the ambivalence of each stage of human experience. Few artists dare to speak like he does of both paternal affection for, and violence against, children. The closeness of his young lovers is balanced by the unbridgeable distance between them. (His contemporary, Edvard Munch, said something similar about human love in coordinated paintings called "Attraction" and "Separation.") In the midst of mid-life this visual panorama of human experience spoke to me.

Just how this experience helped me begin to affirm again the developmental tasks of my own life I realized only partially then. For the moment it was enough to see that, short of death, life is never over. For all of us who are the products of a youth culture, which has trouble affirming the inevitable aging, this was a clear gain. For all of us whose first forty years involved acquiring competence at work, learning to be a spouse and parent, becoming a responsible citizen, it was liberating to discover that there might be more on the mid-life plateau, and beyond. Looking back on it the discovery seems banal: I realized that life goes on! But there was something hidden in the obvious.

Just what this more might be was not clear at the time. (Since I was en route to a fortnight of skiing I thought little more of the sculpture. My concentration was on keeping my weight on the downhill ski!) That it would have to do with neglected, internal cultivation I did not then recognize. For years, it seems, I had been burdened by the felt obligation to be perfect, that is, an utterly loving husband and father, thoroughly intentional about my work, consistent in my behavior. What I needed was to be able to acknowledge not only that I didn't measure up to these absolutes but that I didn't have to. That was the realization which was blocking me, which contributed to my experience of the malaise we call mid-life. I'd had many reminders that I was anything but perfect. Intellectually I knew that it couldn't be otherwise. And I'd often used and heard religious language which emphasized that we are made right with God by grace. But these assurances only began to be convincing as the sculpture dramatized life's ambiguity for me. It was the persistence of inner conflicts which I needed to acknowledge. I had to learn to see these enduring tensions as God-given sources of our vitality as well as our anguish. Rather than expending energy to suppress one side of my internal tensions, I came to see these tensions as sources of strength for new directions of my life. Eventually I was able to visualize the possibility of a lively present as well as a future. (That this did not happen quickly, or with the approval of others to whom I turned, will be discussed later.)

It is by grace, in this instance mediated by pieces of sculpture, that we are able to see and joyfully embrace our conflicted present wholeness. Don't we always experience internal tension between the desires to be dependent and to be independent, between the need to be passive and the need to be aggressive, between our minds and bodies, to say nothing of our feelings and aesthetic sensibilities? Such tensions may be heightened at times of life but they are never wholly absent. To be perfect is not to be without flaw but to be free of the need to pretend flawless-ness. I do not claim that the sculpture caused me to see this. What seems clear is that, at a point when I needed to move beyond a mid-life impasse, when I needed to embrace anew the assurance of God's love for us as we are, Vigeland's work was a catalyst.

I suggest that any vivid encounter with the dynamics of life's stages confronts us with God's call to an inward pilgrimage. Despite the extravagant claims of travel advertisements, few of our trips through the external world contribute very much to our self-understanding. The journeys that matter are through inner space. It is with the relationship of our outer and inner worlds that this book is concerned. Not the notable, celebrated high points but the ordinary, day-to-day interface where we resolve the claims of external pressures and personal needs. It has been my experience that the question of my relationship to God has arisen most vividly from questions generated by my work and my personal relationships. It is in these ordinary aspects of life that God is endlessly calling us to faith by calling us to become more fully ourselves. That it is to self-love that we are called was one of the eventual surprises of that winter afternoon.

An enduring question of my adult life has been this: what is a proper self-love? By proper I mean what acknowledges the needs of the self, one's relationship to others who are both immediate and remote—and the role of these needs and relationships in the life of faith in God. Any less inclusive understanding would sacrifice one or more of life's constituent elements. The question might be put differently: given the triangularity of life—self, others, God—what is the attention to be paid to self which enhances both one's relationships with others and the importance of God in one's life?

Several answers have been given since Jesus' summary of the Commandments: ". . . 'Love the Lord your God with all your heart, with all your soul, with all your mind.' That is the greatest commandment. It comes first. The second is like it: 'Love your neighbor as yourself.' Everything in the Law and the prophets hangs on these two commandments." (Matt. 22:37-40, NEB) In Mark's report Jesus concluded by saying, "There is no commandment greater than these." (Mark 12:31, NEB) Clearly in these obligations to love God, neighbor and self, which are repeated from ancient Law rather than original summations, we have the essence of Jesus' understanding of the Judaism into which he was born.

What remains unclear is the way in which the three elements are to be related. The issue is illumined when we consider the

Greek word, *homaya*, which is translated, "like it." The second Commandment of the summary is said to be like the first. This is misleading. What the word which Matthew uses really means is that the second Commandment is just as great as the first. They are of the same order of importance. Neither may be made subservient to the other. In the triadic life of the believer the relationships to God, to the neighbor and to one's self are of equal value. I suggest that they cannot be understood apart from each other.

The temptation is to resolve the uncertainty created by their equality by giving priority to one of the elements. Following Matthew's insistence that the first is the greatest, love for God has traditionally been given priority. Knowing, as we do, the temptations inherent in both self-love and love for the neighbor this is understandable. It is the basis of much Christian devotion and of the assumption that clarity about God's priority results in proper relationships with the neighbors and oneself.

There are at least two difficulties with this resolution. First, it undermines the dynamic of the triadic relationship. It suggests that by total love for God one necessarily knows how to fulfill relationships to neighbors and self. It assumes one-way traffic only. Must we not say on the basis of the Incarnation that love for God evolves in the course of learning to love one's neighbor and one's self? Only in the course of struggling with the often conflicting claims of others and oneself may love for God be deepened. Second, it violates the equality of the commandments. The first becomes *primus inter pares* rather than one of three equally important relationships. Thus, both because it contradicts scripture and because it threatens to destroy the relationship of equals, this resolution is a temptation.

Fewer have insisted that giving priority to love for the neighbor best maintains the equilateral triangle. Still, this view has had strong defenders and a good case can be made that a loving relationship with one's neighbor properly informs the relationship with God and self. However we must recognize both its lack of scriptural warrant and the danger of this emphasis becoming merely humanistic.

What about a proper self-love as the key to the triadic relationship? It is this temptation of which we may be accused.

The dangers inherent in stressing self-love will seem to some more obvious than either of the alternatives. They are no more nor any less real.

Every effort to simplify the dynamic triad of Jesus' summary of the Law must be refused. Neither love for God nor for the neighbor nor for oneself may be used to regulate others. They are the constituent ingredients of the religious life. No one of them is sufficient unto itself. Neither may be understood apart from the others. No commandment compares in importance with these two and the second is "just as great as the first."

This assertion is both difficult and imperative to affirm. There is no simplification by which one of the commandments always fully informs the others. Every effort to make rigid the obligation to love God, neighbor, and self is an attempt to achieve an un-Biblical simplification which does not maintain the proper demands of the life of faith. Unavoidably, the condition of human life to which the believer aspires involves three variables in endless movement. At any given time the claims of one will be paramount. The needs of the neighbor, as the parable of the Good Samaritan indicates, will sometimes take priority. Alternatively, there are dark nights of the soul when the issues of one's relationship to God must be honored at whatever cost. There are also needs of the self which the believer must learn to love. We may not honor God by dishonoring ourselves. Self-destruction may never be equated with self-sacrifice. The former is the result of hatred for oneself, for which there is no Christian warrant; the latter the fruit of a proper self-love.

The point is that emphases change. For varying periods of time, from a few minutes to a few days or longer, the love of God, neighbor or self will be paramount. This is unavoidable. What is unacceptable is that any transient concentration become normative. Such are the demands of faith that some simplification is endlessly tempting but we must see every simplification as an attempt to escape the work of Christian faith which is to honor equally, by refusing to codify, life's constituent relationships. That the demotion of self love, to which church-goers are often exhorted, results in unwarranted impoverishment of our God-given life I hope to demonstrate.

Of the three elements in the Christian triad it is self-love which has been most suspect. At best it is permitted when all other obligations have been fulfilled. At the worst, self-emptying has been encouraged. Imagine it: that a life, for the salvation of which God is said to have become incarnate and suffered death by crucifixion, is often viewed as unlovable! Something is awry in such an understanding. It is impossible that something for which God would die is of no value. The question is this: how is the believer to value that life to which God has assigned such value? Especially, how is one to love oneself with reference to loving both God and the neighbor whom God also loves.

It will be accomplished, I suggest, by the attention one is able to pay to the particulars of one's life. It is in acknowledging the God-givenness of these particulars that we discover our kinship with our neighbor and that the peril of selfishness is avoided. For selfishness, which many wrongly equate with self-love, is really its antithesis. The root of selfishness is not inordinate self-love. Just the opposite: selfishness is fed by the inability to value one's self. Unaware of the value God gives to human life the selfish person seeks a sense of personal worth which neither acquisitions nor achievements will ever accomplish. There is a pathos in selfishness, however grand its achievements, with which self-love is unfamiliar. Selfishness is engaged in a hopeless undertaking because it is isolated from those relationships which enable the believer to affirm the particulars, however limited, of a God-given life. Ultimately, selfishness is self-destructive; it is never capable of that self-sacrifice which is the final achievement of self-love.

It was to some of the particulars of my life, long neglected but no longer ignorable, that the Vigeland sculpture helped me begin to pay attention. Prone to emphasize the sovereignty of God and obedience to the first commandment, I began to realize that to love God required me to attend to the particulars of my own heart, soul, mind and strength. Not only had I been guilty of a good deal of pretense regarding the completeness of my love; I had been neglectful—perhaps wilfully blind, certainly indifferent—of the ambivalences of my inner life. The sculptor helped me to recognize my own internal mix of good and evil. It was no longer enough to appreciate God's love for what I considered my presentable self. There was another side to me which could no longer be ignored. It came to me—how else can I say it?—that it is the whole person to whom God ascribes value and that it is faith's privilege and responsibility to affirm all that God has already affirmed. It became clear that one dimension of faith is the call to self-love, to become intentional about the mixed particulars of one's life. True love for God is complemented by self-affirmation and the desire to do some good with what limited gifts one actually has. To refuse to acknowledge aspects of one's particularity, to engage in self-deception and to conceal from others, is evidence of bad faith.

With this understanding the work of Christian spirituality becomes three-fold: 1) to be ever more accurately aware of, and grateful for, the strength and limits of one's actual particularities; 2) to affirm as from God one's unrealized potentialities; 3) to desire their good use, and to acknowledge both the deficiency of this desire and one's actual failures. For example, to acknowledge God-given capacities for feelings may rescue one from the God-denying boredom which results from passivity and withdrawal. It does not assure that these feelings will always be constructive. The arousal of anger will generate energies which may enable one to resist some injustice; it may also result in violence against another rather than recognizing something untoward in oneself. The variety of responses to the imprisonment of the hostages in Iran, from a strong patience and willingness to negotiate to those who would have bombed as the only meaningful show of strength, suggests the possibilities when feelings are allowed. The ultimate work of Christian spirituality will be a re-education of our feelings consistent with an understanding of life which affirms the centrality of love for God, neighbor and self.

In the understandings to which I came gradually in the course of mid-life I found it necessary and helpful to pay closer attention to two areas of experience in which I had invested heavily: my vocation and my family. It is these activities to which attention is given in the following chapters. My understandings may be provisional; I do not, however, offer them casually. I do so in twofold hope: that, whatever the limits of my self-perception and candor, some readers may avoid the unnecessary and unproductive isolation I experienced with the onset of mid-life; and that, without minimizing the vast amount which we share with all humankind, to enable some to recognize the personal significance of their unique ordinariness. To be able to affirm the God-givenness of one's particularity, warts and all, is the foretaste of that abundant wholeness which Jesus offers. In his study of the prophets Abraham Heschel puts a related matter clearly.

> What concerns the prophet is the human event as a divine experience. History to us is the record of human experience; to the prophet it is the record of God's experience.[1]

For the person whose sensibilities are informed by the Biblical religions there is no experience in which God does not participate. However necessary it is to stress God's transcendence it must not be emphasized to the point where God is thought only to be "out there."

It is such an understanding which I suggest must be applied to personal experience. Ordinarily we think of a life as a record of private experience. On all counts this is inaccurate. From conception to death we are related to others. At the least we should say that a life is the record of a person's interactions with others. Because of the triadic relationships in Jesus' summary of the Law we must go beyond this: the experiences of a life are part of the record of God's experience. God is present in the limited particulars of each life seeking to accomplish, through the ambivalences of human ordinariness, the good beheld at the completion of the creation.

Nothing less than love for the particulars of our ordinary lives—some grubby, some glorious—will make us agents for good. How society evaluates us is utterly irrelevant. Such evaluations, which are society's primary means of squeezing us into its mold, have this notoriously bad effect: they cause us to become embarrassed and deceiving about our God-given particulars. They undermine our capacity for that self-love which enables us to love our neighbor. The confidence we seek for affirming ourselves in mid-life must come not from the continued effort to conform to society's evaluations, but rather, it must be grounded in our particular God-givenness. In this sense we may affirm mid-life as yet another of God's gifts which we must learn to love. Whether or not that loving process is underway is determined by the attention we are able to pay to ourselves and to those around us. It is never a matter of looking but one way.

CHAPTER 2

Mid-life: Looking Both Ways

One of the lessons which we learned as children had to do with crossing the street. The first step towards freedom was our demonstrated ability to look both ways and to calculate our chances accurately before we stepped off of the side-walk. Being a surviving pedestrian is, in many ways, analogous to the experience of mid-life. Unlike the young, who look mostly ahead, or the aged, who are often nostalgically preoccupied, the person in mid-life seems caught in the middle of a two-way street. Both past and future make claims: the needs of aging parents may be as urgent as those of adolescent children. People in this situation may rightly feel sandwiched between the imperious claims of both older and younger generations. When so caught, one looks occasionally with envy at those who seem to be on one-way streets. The traffic seems more orderly and, for the young, faster. That it is often duller, like Inter-State driving, is less readily recognized.

Like all analogies this one becomes misleading. Learning to survive as a pedestrian suggests that growing up is primarily a negative matter of avoiding dangers. Despite the tendency of many people to view mid-life in this way, I propose a much more positive understanding of the opportunities for those who are no longer young and not yet old. They may range in age from thirty to sixty. The precise chronology doesn't matter because it is not identifiable by year. What does matter is the onset of certain experiences which may be as terrifying when first encountered as was crossing the street by oneself for the first time. It will be tempting to deny the need to move until one discovers, as did the hesitant child, that the enjoyment of the future depends upon the ability to handle the present. To have access to experience beyond the safety of one's block, the child must learn to look both ways, to calculate the risks, and to step forth. It is unfortunate that at a time when men and women often begin to yearn for a simpler life, the process of mid-life maturation begins with an enlargement of responsibilities. The nature of the enlargement is the surprise.

As we have said, those in mid-life are often responsible for people who are both older and younger. These are never casual concerns and we must appreciate the anguish of those who live with them. It is not, however, my present purpose to dwell on obligations to aging parents and children. Rather, I want to suggest that to embrace one's mid-life involves a responsibility to oneself as well as to others. Needed throughout life and often neglected, this self-cultivation involves the development of abilities both to anticipate one's future and to reach back into the past. It is the urgency of and the potential for this which are heightened in the middle years. At mid-life the route to renewal begins by embracing in oneself the needs long served in others. There is both a hidden child and an aged adult within each mid-life person. The temptation to reach in only one direction will be abandoned only when we admit that mid-life is a two-way street. Especially bewildering may be the realization that the dangers, and the opportunities, come from both directions!

It may seem an impossible assignment, and one may find oneself getting into the weirdest psychic positions, but is there an alternative? Having been largely future-oriented for years, being not yet old but increasingly appreciative of the past, one must learn to look both ways and to calculate all the risks in order to be able to move. The tension persists between the security of past achievements and the uncertainty of our potential for future development. We are always poised between memory and hope, searching for the proper combination of both for the sake of a vivid present life. It is a balancing act during which the rope is at times firm and the combination comes easily; at other times it goes slack and our balance is threatened. Youth may be more disposed to risking but this capacity, when it isn't foolhardiness, is always related to a sense of security. Age may clutch security more firmly but, if this very security is not to be destroyed, age must be able to risk anew by remembering the rewards of risks previously taken. The endless task of the present, of which mid-life is a heightened illustration, is to be in touch with both one's assuring memories and risky hopes yet to be realized.

It is these transitional stages, these two-way streets, in the life-cycle which represent the times of greatest opportunity and threat. Throughout our lives there is both a yesterday remembered and a tomorrow anticipated. Change is constant. Usually we recall and anticipate little more than a day or two at a time; occasionally, as in the course of a holiday or an illness, we encompass larger blocks of experience; a few times in our lives we have the opportunity to deal with major milestones. These markers, when the tasks of a particular era are as best completed as they can presently be and we are ready to move on to new tasks, are called the life stage transitions. Like many changes of direction they are dangerous and full of promise.

The temptation is to equate these transitions with external changes. Thus, the onset of puberty is identified as the beginning of adolescence, a fortieth (or some other) birthday as the arrival of mid-life, graying hair as the signal of aging. While there is often some correlation between such external factors and one's development, the emphasis on the external is misleading. The dynamics of human growth are not simply equatable with exterior signs. Progress from one stage to the next is primarily internal. There may be accompanying external evidences of change but they are no proof that the progress suggested has been or is being accomplished. A person of sixty years may still be working through issues of adolescence; an adolescent may have begun to come to terms with human finitude more wisely than the elder on a death bed. Such circumstances may not be typical but they are not impossible. It is this realization which char-acterizes contemporary thinking about the stages through which lives pass: mere chronological aging does not assure maturation. Maturity results from the internal embrace of appropriate elements of one's past and one's future. That this involves the ability to acknowledge the inseparability of gains and losses is one of the qualities characteristic of maturity. That you cannot have gains only is one fact which makes avoidance of maturation tempting. In order that we may have a feeling for the trauma which increasing numbers of people experience in mid-life I want to report two descriptions of normative human development.

Erik H. Erikson has probably done more than any other single person to acquaint us with the potential for growth which continues from birth to death. While we shall wait until the next chapter to describe his understanding of the stages of normal human development, it is essential to know that at each stage we are pulled in both positive and negative directions. It will also be useful to know how he describes the final goal of integrity towards which lives should move. It is integrity which should predominate, although some elements of despair and disgust will persist. It is theoretically possible that a person might possess integrity as a young adult; that is, might have fashioned an identity adequate to enable intimacy and a genuinely generative attitude towards the future. However, it is more typically later in life that one confronts the issues of integrity and despair. On clinical and anthropological evidence Erikson describes the following attributes of integrity.

> It is the acceptance of one's own and only life cycle and of the people who have become significant to it as something that had to be and that, by necessity, permitted of no substitutions. It thus means a new different love of one's parents, free of the wish that they should have been different, and an acceptance of the fact that one's life is one's own responsibility. It is a sense of comradeship with men and women of distant times and of different pursuits, who have created orders and objects and sayings conveying human dignity and love. Although aware of the relativity of all the various life styles which have given meaning to human striving, the possessor of integrity is ready to defend the dignity of his own life style against all physical and economic threats. For he knows that an individual life is the accidental coincidence of but one life cycle with but one segment of history; and that for him all human integrity stands and falls with the one style of integrity of which he partakes.[1]

While the presence of despair is often recognizable by fear of death, the sense that time is running out is less important to despair than the inextinguishable wish that one had lived differently. Some of these despairing elements will be found in even the healthiest integrity but they will not be the person's distinguishing quality.

For a somewhat different, and equally useful, characterization of normative human development we turn to an important book by Catholic literary critic W. F. Lynch.

> Some medical men would say that learning to tolerate ambivalence is a decisive struggle for the sick in their conquest of hopelessness. Such a position tallies remarkably, though analogically, with the findings and goals of true religion.
>
> By ambivalence, in this sense, we mean a number of things: the ability to accept negative and unpleasant feelings as well as positive and pleasant ones; the end of a life of habitual denial, because now when one loves he need not deny the drawbacks and the difficulties. Decision now becomes possible, because formerly decision had been impeded by the unconscious negative feelings that went with it: the wish not to do a thing as well as the wish to do it. Now a man can commit himself strongly . . . to things without needing to believe that there must be no negatives and that he must be in the constant presence of absolute thoughts and feelings. I can choose more freely, knowing well that another's contrary choice might be just as good as mine.[2]

Common to both writers are the assumptions that there is a direction in which lives should be heading and that the worst hindrance to such movement is the tendency to think in absolutistic terms. For Erikson integrity is the goal but, as with the negative at all of the life-stages, this is achieved by the subordination of despair rather than its elimination from one's life. Lynch wants people to be capable of making and sustaining meaningful commitments and recognizes the ability to embrace one's ambivalences, rather than the need to suppress and deny them, as the quality necessary for such achievement. The paradox is clear: single-mindedness, especially because of the pretense it inevitably involves, assures failure to reach any mature goal. Since all such goals are inherently complex—for

instance the tensions in Erikson's integrity between self-affirmation and empathy with others—it is inappropriate to demand
an unequivocal attitude toward any such goal. While equivocation must be transcended for one to be able to act, two things
should be noted. First, that greater patience with equivocation
may often result in wiser action. It would have made little sense
to me twenty years ago but I am beginning to appreciate the
wisdom attributed to the Buddha: "Don't just do something;
stand there!" Second, because we are at least as complex as the
goals to which we aspire some negative elements will persist in
any resolve to act. That is simply the human condition and to
believe otherwise will be endlessly misleading and fatiguing.

It may be unfair to compare such sophisticated understandings of normative human growth with the following popular
statements which I have chosen to represent more normal
experience. The latter, however, suggests the extent to which
ordinary people are trapped in socially-derived aspirations to
which they never gave conscious assent, including the
fulfillment of goals which were largely foisted onto them by an
economy of abundance. Whether or not such abundance , or the
behavior required to assure it, would contribute to their
maturation is a question rarely asked before it is too late. The
question becomes possible only after the disillusionment has
begun. By this time the range of one's obligations may make it
difficult, or impossible, to embrace the Buddha's advice. The
question and lament with which the following concludes is not
the cry of a rare individual in mid-life.

> What are my living circumstances? What do you want me to tell
> you, Doc? I wake up at three in the morning; I feel paunchy and
> tired. I look at my wife snoring next to me with two pounds of
> makeup smeared all over her face. Both my kids, God bless them,
> are inches taller than I am. Both tell me that I'm square and a
> supporter of a hypocritical society. Big deal. I then think of the
> job, and I just know they're gonna make Harry executive
> vice-president and not me. My secretary will be consoling, always
> trying to get my attention. Stupid broad. You can't get involved in
> the office. Weekends I play golf at the country club, have a couple
> of drinks, go home, eat, watch TV, play cards with the neighbors,
> hear a little gossip, go to bed, go to work. Come next August I'll be

thirty-seven. I often wonder, 'How is this different from what my old man and my mother used to do?' Except their way of life wasn't as expensive as mine. They were never as much in hock as I am. Things aren't at all the way I thought they would be. Sometimes I think: to hell with it all! But I can't just run out. What the hell do I do?[3]

As one would expect from a former chairman of the F.C.C., Nicholas Johnson's language is more esoteric than is that of the person just quoted. Further, Johnson has both a more adequate vision of the potential for human development and an analysis of the "corporate interlock" which contributes so much to the entrapment of Americans at mid-life.

Living ought to be individual, spontaneous, extemporaneous, a personal quest, evolution, an experience in uniqueness. But living your life according to the corporate plan involves no more of a creative 'centering' . . . than painting in numbered spaces with the indicated colors is 'art'. . . .

The corporate interlock of jobs, products, and life style means that once you come into the circle at any point you find yourself surrounded by all of it. And once you're in it it's very difficult to get a little bit out. The choices remaining to you are relatively meaningless . . . And from the corporate layers of externals comes your very identity—and the smothering of your soul.

The corporate interlock involves the unquestioned assumptions in our lives. Because they are unquestioned, and largely unperceived, it is difficult enough to describe individual examples even one at a time. But the point of the interlock is that they are not just individual examples but part of a pattern—the test pattern television is reinforcing in millions of us hour after hour.[4]

At one level Johnson's identification of the "corporate interlock" helps to explain the lament of the mid-life interviewee previously quoted. Unwittingly, perhaps, but in all likelihood eagerly, that man stepped onto a treadmill from which he finds himself unable to step off. And, were he able to exit, there is no evidence in the interview that he could embrace Johnson's vision of life as ". . . individual, spontaneous, extemporaneous, a personal quest . . . an experience in uniqueness." We shall want to assess Johnson's individualism later, which I suspect needs a corporate dimension which does not imply an "interlock," but immediately we must try to see how the society exploits the vulnerability of adolescence in ways which eventually produce the cry of mid-life, "What the hell do I do?"

There are at least two major periods in our lives, adolescence and mid-life, when we are especially capable of change. These opportune times for growth involve issues which are primarily internal. Further, there is such an intimate relationship between adolescent experiences and those of mid-life that the latter may be viewed, in part, as a recurrence of the former. We might entitle this section mid-life adolescence.

To explain this assertion about mid-life, which I view as at least as much an occasion for celebration as for regret, we must first understand some of the ingredients of the developmental stage which we call adolescence. So powerful are the changes taking place during those years, and so unacceptable is some of the behavior of which youth are capable, that it is often difficult for older people to appreciate both the struggles which are going on and the pain involved. The fragile beauty of the process is often obscured both by the embarassed young person and by the inability of elders to see other than the bizarre and the frightening.

There are at least four ingredients in those transitional teenage years: its modernity; its experience of limitations and relativity, both of which are aggravated by our emphasis on decisions; its vulnerability to societal lures; and its peculiar temptation. How all this is related to the fundamental physiological changes of puberty we shall discuss later. For now, however, let me indicate that I take puberty's changes with great seriousness. As they are the original cause of personal dislocation, I suspect that they are also key to any eventual relocations.

First, we note that the protracted phenomenon we call adolescence is a very modern development. Children have always come to sexual maturity, often at a later chronological age than is true today. Rites of passage, which we largely lack, were developed in all societies to acknowledge the coming of age. Adulthood was conferred upon those able to pass through what was often a very demanding ritual.

Distinctive of adolescence as a modern phenomenon, which Rousseau was among the first to recognize, is the fact that the society's role is decreasingly explicit. Adult status, which included both a designated job and the selection of a spouse by tribe or family, is not something which any agency in our society is able to confer. It is true that we withhold certain privileges from youth, for instance the right to be licensed to drive, legal voting and drinking ages, but the arrival of the entitling birthdate hardly accomplishes what was achieved by the *rites de passage*. It is the privilege and burden of today's adolescents to make decisions about basic matters which will have enduring influence on their lives. It is the fact of their formal freedom to choose a career, a mate if such is their desire, and the values and affiliations by which to live which is distinctive to contemporary American youth and young adults. While there is no necessity to continue in one's parents' work or value-commitments, and while there are few parent-determined marriages, two reservations must be entered in youth's behalf: such an amount of freedom is not an unmixed blessing; and, there are a variety of ways by which society sees to it that youth exercise their formal freedom in ways that parents and other significant elders can approve. The burden of freedom and the means by which society encourages conformity, then, are the next characteristics of adolescence to be considered.

One of the experiences of adolescence is the gradual, occasionally rapid, erosion of many of the certainties of childhood. Subject to awesome changes in one's body, changes which indicate clearly that one is no longer a child without giving assurance that one will become an adult, the adolescent unavoidably looks both ways. Perhaps most disconcerting to parents whose first child is coming of age is the adolescent's ability not only to look but to move quickly, and often without apparent cause, both forward and backward. The vacillation between assertions of independence and the child-like need to be comforted is often too much, even for well-meaning parents. Two of the crucial skills which few parents acquire without some injury to all concerned is to know when to hold on imperceptibly, and when to let go without resentment or rejection. That the ability is transferable to marital relationships is but one of the possible benefits of having been a parent.

But it is not primarily parents who are unsettled by the adolescent's attraction both to the past and to the future. This time of high potential and pain is characterized by a yearning both for the certainties which are being eroded and for the, as yet unachievable, status of adulthood. William G. Perry of Harvard's Bureau of Study Counsel has paid careful attention to some of the stages of vacillation ordinarily experienced during the college years. Parents and young adults would benefit from his reminders of the successive bewilderment, skepticism and resolution through which most students pass as the certainties of childhood give way before the relativism of modern knowledge. Perry wisely recognizes that such intellectual awakening is never without complications for the total life of the person and rarely fails to influence all his or her significant relationships. The burden of adolescent freedom is borne primarily but not exclusively by the young person.[5]

Adolescence is a stage of life in which it is impossible to know all that is needed in order to be able to make basic decisions. The impossibility arises both from the limitations of the learner and from the fact that even all knowledge, were one able to acquire it, would not make possible a choice free of all arbitrariness. This is the nature of the epistemological impasse in which we live. But, on what basis is arbitrariness possible? The often silent cry of the adolescent is as profound as that of the interviewee who asked, "What the hell do I do?" Their circumstances may be quite dissimilar but it is only the form of the student's question which is different: "In a world in which any course of action is as valid and as invalid as any other, how do I choose?!" Perry has some perceptive observations about the role of faculty in this situation. He recognizes that part of what students seek in relationships with their teachers is some clue as to how it is possible for people with so much education to make a commitment to any one area of work. In other words, how does one live with recognized imperfection?

While I have little doubt that good teachers have long helped young people to discover their own answers, I suspect that a more fundamental relationship than that of student-teacher is central to most resolutions of the adolescent's burden of freedom. We need to see that it is society as a whole that has ways of encouraging youth to move beyond the indecisiveness of relativism. This fact is obscured by the tendency in all discussions of adolescence to give the impression that young men and women exist apart from society. Partly, perhaps, because they often don't know where they do or will fit in, it is tempting to view them as exiles. That, I believe, would be a serious error. They may not have a present place but they do hope for one in the not-too-remote future. Therein lies society's opportunity, which is the third ingredient of adolescence we are considering.

Clearly, it is the responsibility of every society to create the conditions whereby its young people may gradually come to see that there will be adult places for them to occupy. To have failed to create such conditions for a sizeable number of its youth, as seemed to be the case in the 1960's, does great harm to vulnerable adolescents and invites revolutionary changes. However threatening this may be to the self-interest of the privileged it is imperative that we see such movements as efforts on the part of youth and their allies to create a society in which there will be opportunities for employment, family-making, and meaningful participation in public life. Can we deny that these are among the conditions for survival and self-respect increasingly desired throughout the world? There is much to admire in the efforts of young people to claim greater responsibility for their own lives and for the future of their society. The potential for tragedy in such efforts has been powerfully suggested in the Jamaican film, *The Harder They Come*.

Like all societies, ours must have a climate which permits youth to look with hope to the future. For reasons which included both the Civil Rights Movement and opposition to the Vietnam War, it was this climate which became doubtful for many young people in the 1960's. Aware of the racial injustices in the society and perceiving the arrogant folly of our involvement in Southeast Asia, the disaffections ranged from informed moral outrage to the self-destructiveness of the drug culture. The traditional, middle-class lures failed to capture many youths' imaginations. That this was an occasion for euphoria for some observers was nowhere better seen than in Charles Reich's book, *The Greening of America*. A decade later little of the political vitality of the '60's has endured and there is even less of the greening optimism. Youth are again amenable to the traditional lures. This means both that the turbulence of adolescence is less troubling to their elders and that we may predict a turbulent mid-life for today's youth. But that is to get ahead of the characterization of adolescence which is being sketched.

We indicated above that adolescence is that time when, needing to know more than one can to choose wisely and yearning to acquire the adult status which the society no longer confers by any rites, young people are open to the assurances of their society. For us this often results in an emphasis on work, education, and the importance of early career decisions; all with the assurance that fulfilling rewards come to those who comply. For many youth it is a believable promise. Having been encouraged since grade school to consider the many avenues of employment open to those who are qualified; having had reinforced from all quarters the direct connection between level of education and future success; having discovered the reasonably consistent link between academic effort and grades; many youth are able to commit themselves to lives of hard work with the prospect of deferred gratifications.

It would be foolish to decry this formula. Much of its emphasis is sound and for many it has been the route to success. But there are deficiencies and dangers. The formula promises more than it can give to all its adherents. Among the un- or under-employed there are holders of PhDs. Driving a taxi in Cambridge, Massachusetts, after his college education a young man jokingly observed that he was under-qualified. "You really should have a 'Masters' to cab in this town!" Further, the formula encourages a largely instrumental attitude toward education. While this is especially noxious in a liberal arts environment where, in the nature of that liberating process, one must give oneself to the material, the fact is that such colleges are increasingly inclined to justify themselves on the basis of their vocational utility. It is not a matter of being hostile to questions of usefulness; that would be foolish. Rather I am concerned about the long-range and varied utility of a college education rather than the immediate gains for which the manipulative aspire.

Such an instrumental approach to education undermines the formation of a conscience that enables the privileged to do some good for the society as well as doing well by themselves. Character-formation may not be in vogue today but can any society long endure if it is indifferent to the values of those being trained to occupy its most sensitive and best rewarded positions? Finally, the formula by which youth are being lured presupposes a split between intellect and feeling, between work and love. Since we are not inherently schizoid this is always a dangerous presupposition. It is diabolical today because it is often suggested that these primary aspects of our lives not only should be kept separate but that this can be done with impunity. Since emotional life is less controllable, and therefore the source of inefficient diversions, many youth are willing to believe the assurances that the split is without consequences and the development of affectionate relationships is postponable. It is, I trust, possible to see here some of the sources of both the interviewee's cry and the state of the "corporate interlock." Youth who subscribe uncritically to the formula have, to an unsuspected degree, abandoned Nicholas Johnson's vision of life as ". . . an experience of uniqueness." The seeds have been sown which may issue in the unforeseen lament, "What the hell do I do?"

The final ingredient of adolescence is the most difficult to defend. It is the peculiar temptation of that stage of life to conceal its vulnerability in the pretended strength of adulthood. For reasons which all can recall and understand, youth elects to suppress uncertainties about the future in favor of the certainty of a career. Do not misunderstand. I recognize both the inevitability and the desirability of particular commitments. It is sheer romanticism to idolize vulnerability and uncertainty. Rather, I want to stress three interrelated facts which make it possible to see the traumas of mid-life as the consequence of acquiescence to the unique temptation of adolescence. First, in order to achieve the required career clarity it is necessary both to elevate work above love and to devalue aspects of one's self which are not immediately vocationally relevant. Secondly, since work is not as inherently fulfilling as the formula led one to believe, there is a gradual questioning of its demands. Finally, since aspects of the self may be temporarily suppressed but not obliterated, what we call mid-life is a deep cry from within to acknowledge parts of one's self which may have been ignored since adolescence.

Because it is a time of considerable dislocation and pain it is tempting to view mid-life negatively and to try to avoid its anguishes. But may it not be the crucial effort of something to be born? I am persuaded that even the best possible transitions from adolescence are imperfect. It is impossible to take adequate account of all aspects of the self. Those who subscribe determinedly to the societal formula may become unable to hear the internal voices of mid-life. Unlike more vulnerable people they may be unshaken, but at what cost? Uncritical embrace of the formula may result in "success," which I understand to require the approval of others. Not only does such an embrace not assure a sense of fulfillment, which involves self-approbation; it often creates major barriers to it. It is this desire to be able to assent to one's own life which marks the onset of mid-life. No longer does applause satisfy as it once did. That this may first be experienced as a trauma is a reminder of how formidable are the barriers to self-reacquaintance which will have to be dismantled.

Perhaps a simple illustration would be useful. Sigurd Olson, naturalist and writer in his eighties, insists that it is the capacity for wonder which keeps a person young. That most children have the capacity is one of the reasons people are attracted to them. A child's ability to be fascinated by almost anything—flowers, a piece of fabric, an animal; but especially its interest in a face, a finger, or a foot—is precious. Despite the knowledge and experience of adulthood, despite our apparent ability to control the environment, that sense of wonder should not be lost. It is a source of enjoyment, of a sense of oneself and of one's relationship to the larger world. That little of such delight persists in many adults, many of whom are deeply bored, is a source of the trauma of mid-life. To recover a capacity for wonder, so often lost during decades of purposeful busyness, is a proper desire of the middle years.

In addition to the fact that the potential changes of mid-life are primarily internal, notice must be taken of four additional characteristics: it is a period of life in which certain issues may first emerge; whether or not it is a universal phenomenon its work is complicated by distinctive features of our society; it holds the potential for important review and evaluation; finally, it is a heightened opportunity for greater intentionality. Where possible we shall try to show the connections between these mid-life meanings and those which characterize adolescence.

The transitional stage of mid-life would seem to be universal. Unlike adolescence, which required for its appearance many developments of modern life, all people have passed through experiences of aging not unlike those known today. (Not all societies have formalized the transition as clearly as has Hinduism where, upon the completion of a man's years as householder, family-maker, worker, citizen, he is expected to abandon these responsibilities in favor of the search for enlightenment.) Many natural factors undoubtedly contribute to the gradual realization that one is no longer young and that there are realities beyond those of making and acquiring with which one must begin to come to terms. Just what these additional realities are may be initially unclear.

What is clear is that societies vary in helping persons both to identify the mid-life agenda and to get on with its work. From birth we are deeply influenced by the prevailing attitudes of the world around us. While many such attitudes and values are consciously held and publicly discussed these are probably not as important to our actual behavior as are those that are subtly built into the structures. Every society gives better support to some groups than to others. Isn't this what the protests against racism and sexism and ageism are all about? Aren't they efforts to correct traditional preferences given to young, white males? The difficulty we have trying to imagine transplanting to the American scene the attitudes and aspirations of Hinduism says a great deal about us. We are neither clear about the proper business of people at mid-life nor do we give much support to those who understand that business in the light of the inevitability of aging. Perhaps the accumulation of years is the one acquisition with which the acquisitive society is unsympathetic.

The universal fact of mid-life, then, is significantly complicated for us by factors reasonably specific to this society. Two of
these seem particularly important: our emphasis on the
quantitative and external and our understanding of human
strength. Both of these compound the difficulty of mid-life: the
former by having limited tolerance for internal considerations;
the latter by its reluctance to embrace the simultaneity of gains
and losses. The fact that our perception of human growth is
largely quantitative and external gives a peculiar twist to our
experience of mid-life. That this is a time of life when the
quantitative model may first be questioned identifies the
problem; that there is little appreciation for any other model
compounds it. I am not suggesting that a concern for the
measurable is wrong. My complaint is that we have converted a
legitimate and important aspect of reality into an ideology. Not
only does our preoccupation with quantity underlie much of our
desperate acquisitiveness but we are increasingly unable to
appreciate any other dimension of human experience. The
quantitative preoccupation which was inimical to a sound
negotiation of adolescence has the potential for being lethal at
mid-life. So much of what's important to the development of
human lives is ignored by a singular preoccupation with only
external considerations. The cry of the mid-life man quoted
earlier, "What the hell do I do?" did not arise from a rich inner
life. It was from an emptiness cluttered with quantities of things
that the lament came.

At the public level a competence in quantitative matters is
obviously important. This should not obscure the fact, however,
that limitless technical skill does not assure social justice.
Quantitative facts do not yield humane policy. They are the raw
material with which just policy may be fashioned but
judgements about values and priorities are unavoidable.
Informed personal conviction is the qualitative stuff of public
life. How the limited pie of resources is cut is not determined by
the quantitative model. You cannot derive values from facts, no
matter how many of the latter you accumulate.

At the personal level the perils of the quantitative model
should be more obvious. Nobody should be deceived about the
inability of wealth or power to enhance the quality of one's life.

But, despite the cupidity of corporate executives and the various Watergates, most of us still aspire to more of everything. The "best" of students, those most dedicated to the formula, become incapable of assenting to their own lives except in terms of the grades which others assign to their work. The irony is that no quantity of "A's" sustains such a person's sense of worth. Endlessly more of same are required until it may finally dawn on them that the formula just doesn't work. Something other than quantity and external approval is needed. A recently published study of happiness indicates what some have long known, that the appetite for things is insatiable. The only apparent satisfaction in having something is to desire more of the same. The treadmill is endless.[6]

The consequences of this for human development are frightening. Appreciation of internal struggles and the qualitative growth which result from the interplay of the self with the wider reality is either never acquired or soon lost. For example, the adolescent immobilized by awareness of the relativity of all knowledge, who may therein be approaching depths of his or her own being from which creativity emerges, is urged quickly out of such a state by some external act such as declaring a major or by identifying with some pre-professional group. The issue is internal, the solution external; the issue qualitative, the solution quantitative. The growth, admittedly painful, which might have occurred is aborted by denying that such perplexities are inherent to human experience and maturation.

The young person who accepts this route of concealment—and what alternatives are there which are well represented?—has made a commitment which requires him/her to concentrate exclusively on external and quantitative matters. The accumulation of courses and degrees, the size of salary, the rapidity of promotions, the large house of one's dreams, the personal appearance of one's spouse, the achievements of one's children, the remoteness or the costliness of one's vacations, are the ingredients of the "corporate interlock." One may never ask about the social usefulness of one's work or the degree to which it fulfills. In our society who ponders the effects of tourism on Third World countries and people? The focus is always outward and quantitative. The answer to every question is to acquire more of something—almost anything will do.

The ignored effect of externalization is to distance people from themselves. People often don't know what they think or feel until some authority tells them. We are out of touch with our inner lives. It may seem strange to put it this way but, if one is fortunate, the alienation becomes intolerable. This is the gift of mid-life. It is the realization that there is more to one's life than the formula has allowed one to cultivate. It is the realization that, however satisfying one's work and relationships have been, neither career nor marriage and family—nor the combination— will fulfill one's life. It may have been necessary to believe that they would to enable us to move out of the impasse of adolescence. And the achievements which they have made possible remain important. But there is an almost universal tendency to overburden such experiences with expectations which they cannot fulfill. It's as though we had been led to believe that by keeping ourselves endlessly busy we could escape the need to cultivate our own lives, as though an abundance of the external would substitute for the absence of an inner life, as though one's work load determined one's sense of self-worth. Some apparently think that frenzied schedules fashion such inwardness. That busyness and acquisitions only temporarily conceal the lack of a center is apparent at the point at which we begin to ask, abundance for what? Like adolescence, mid-life is another major opportunity to encounter the question of meaning.

C. G. Jung observed that this was the question being asked by most of his middle-aged patients. Rollo May reports similar symptoms. The problems which Freud took to be universal prove to have had their origins more in the rigidities of bourgeois Vienna than in any enduring sexual complexes. If what I take to be the evidence of contemporary therapists is accurate I sense an additional, complicating issue: many of those who are today perplexed about the meaning of their lives are much younger than the middle-aged who came to Jung in Zurich. Some experience of disillusionment seems to be occurring to men and women in their late twenties. Disturbing is the fact that some young people are abandoning the illusions about work, family and public life before they have had the opportunity to discover some of the relative gains of those important life experiences. This results in the need to grapple with ultimate issues without the relative strength that comes from having experienced some success and failure in one's career, as a spouse and parent, and in some phase of citizenship. For example, I believe that in my encounter with some of the mid-life issues I was better able to cope because I knew that I had done some things moderately well. At nothing had I been a flaming success but I knew that I had given something of myself to my work, to my wife and children, and to the society and had been rewarded for my efforts. At none of these had I done as well as I might once have dreamed about doing. However, I had learned some important survival lessons from experiences into which I had been lured by societal illusions. Very ordinary experiences of success and failure, that were made possible by commitment to some basic illusions, also proved to be the basis on which I gradually saw that it was possible to understand my life in a new way without necessarily abandoning the commitments. Another of the important lessons was the discovery that few failures are fatal. Both others and I survived situations in which I simply lacked the relevant skills and/or the appropriate will. Often my limitation proved to be the occasion in which others drew upon unrecognized resources. In other words, I discovered both that I wasn't perfect and that for life to continue—sometimes even to thrive—it was not necessary for me to be so. I neither could nor needed to be all-sufficient. The feeling is not unlike that described by John Berryman when he wrote: ". . . I am still here, severely damaged, but functioning."[7]

My point is simple: if people are experiencing the disillusionment at ever earlier times of life they will lack some of the traditional resources with which their forebears made their way through the troubled agenda of mid-life. Just to have had these traditional experiences does not assure painless negotiation of this agenda. But they do provide perspectives on self and others which are relevant to the somewhat new developmental work of the middle years. To what extent those who abandon illusions prematurely will be attracted to simplistic "solutions" to life's perplexities I do not know. Perhaps the resource possessed by those whose adult experience has been traditional is the realization that there are no simple answers. The instruction of traditional adulthood is that you win some and lose some and that this is not fatal!

It is likely that those who lead untraditional lives will tend to be only forward-looking. Lacking sufficient positive and negative experiences of adulthood, they will be little inclined to look both ways at mid-life. That they will lack continuity is no less serious a deficiency in the middle years than it is in adolescence. The point of Erikson's emphasis on identity formation is not that the adolescent must create something wholly new. Creation *ex nihilo* is better left to the Bible where it is a profoundly important myth. The adolescent's task, in response to deep changes which take place at puberty, is to fashion a sense of self which embraces both what one has been and what one may become. The key to the success of this process is not the orginality of the adolescent's self-design but the extent to which the design is confirmable by those people who are important to the adolescent's life. A successful adolescence incorporates puberty's changes into the person one has been in a way that makes for a believable future. The mid-life task is similar: one should incorporate the changes of the middle years in such a way that one's hopes for the future are consonant with both present reality and personal history. The achievement of a satisfying balance between productivity and pleasure, useful-ness and enjoyment, will vary with individuals. The task is to make adequate provision for both.

The second of the culture-specific factors which complicate the mid-life transition for many Americans can be introduced by a brief quotation from the distinguished psychoanalyst Erich Fromm, who recognizes the interrelationship of social attitudes and individual health.

> . . . most people do not admit to themselves feelings of fear, boredom, loneliness, hopelessness—that is to say, they are unconscious of these feelings. Our social pattern is such that the successful man is not supposed to be afraid or bored or lonely. . . . In order to have the best chance for promotion he must repress fear as well as doubt, depression, boredom, or hopelessness.[8]

While such concealment and pretense is not healthy for anybody, it may make impossible the growth which inheres in mid-life. For reasons which go back at least to frontier self-reliance, our capacity for personal development is restrained by our limited understanding of the varieties of human strength. We are the prisoners of a misguided sense of adulthood which blocks our appreciation both for our inner ambivalences and for the inseparability of gains and losses throughout life. Since these are inherent tensions no amount of denial renders them inoperative. We can only use energies, which could be more profitably spent elsewhere, to conceal their presence from others and, at the worst, from ourselves. By mid-life this often becomes quite fatiguing.

Before proceeding I should make clear that I do not assume that complete honesty, an utter lack of pretense, is possible. What is possible is a life directed towards greater self-awareness and progressive freedom from pretense. In general I am convinced that it is the direction of one's life that makes for a sense of fulfillment. This, of course, is the antithesis of the prevailing quantitative attitude which tends to assume that it matters little where one is headed as long as it is at high speed.

Whatever the historical roots may be of our *machismo*, the immediate source of our confusion about strength and weakness lies in our attitude towards adolescence. As we have indicated, this is a period of life marked by extreme vulnerability. Lacking the innocence of childhood and not yet recognized as an adult, the young person exists in limbo. While such a non-status is unavoidably disquieting, it is made intolerable primarily by the fear it arouses in surrounding adults. That adults were not always as apprehensive about these transitional years is one of the things we need to re-discover. Was, for example, the *wanderjahr* not encouraged precisely by the recognition that young people need a wider range of experience in order to be able to discover what they wish to do? Underlying this attitude would seem to have been the sound recognition that, where freedom of career-choice was involved, it took time to know enough both about oneself and about the world to be able to settle on a career. This, which may have been the model for Erikson's endorsement of a moratorium for youth and which is not unrelated to such programs as VISTA and the Peace Corps, seems much wiser than our anxious determination to have youth identify a career goal before they know very much about either themselves or the world. Our behaviour suggests that adults are actively uncomfortable with youth's freedom to choose their area of work. Apparently we want to have it both ways: that they be free and that they make up their minds early. The pattern of parental pressures suggests that the latter is the preference. (Two things should be noted in passing: first, the impression given to children, often by the schools, that they may become whatever they will is at least misleading. For reasons arising from the incompatibility of some people with some jobs youth's freedom is not absolute. Second, the impression is often given to students that the career for which they prepare determines the work which they will eventually do. Actually few people today continue for the rest of their lives in their first job. From my own life I can report that, as an undergraduate, I was quite unaware of the existence of the work in which I have been engaged for decades.)

The wise choice of a career is a complex and subtle process for which time must be allowed. We have been victimized by the substitution of career for the concept of vocation. The latter took seriously the importance of a proper "fit" between a person and his or her work. In the career-mania which we impose on youth we seem to be guided by the fear that unless one gets an early start the race will be lost. The imagery of all this is bad and, to the extent that it is successfully imposed upon adolescents, it is almost bound to make mid-life traumatic. Who does not know the mid-life "loser" who won all the early races? Or, more rarely, the unsuccessful person who comes to life for the first time in middle age? The attitude that youth must be discouraged from uncertainty is unfortunate. From the vulnerability of adolescence we rush them to the temporary invulnerability of a career-choice. About the short-range gains of such a process there need be little quarrel. The young person who knows the intended career can more easily choose courses, determine a major, get on with fellowship applications and graduate schools. The system is predicated on such efficiency and immediately serves well those who can conform to it. What it requires is either the luck of a good fit, which does happen, or the ability of the person to tuck into the job without complaint. Since luck is hardly universal the system calls for what we call strength, that is, a lot of concealment and pretense. The ability to be satisfied by the system's quantitative rewards is the strength which we nurture. That we are unable to distinguish between patience and resignation goes unnoticed and unlamented!

Thus is youth often persuaded to pretend a certainty which it lacks. For many the uncertainty is to be overcome, or concealed, by hard work. For some, at least temporarily, the adaptation works. Their efforts are rewarded and they increasingly identify with their chosen roles. Where hard work fails there is but one recognized remedy: even harder work. Whatever the problem—grief, boredom, depression, fear—we have but one solution: "Get busy!" That the source of such problems might be yearnings for deeper self-acquaintance we cannot admit. The need to appear strong, either by certainty in one's role or by work-diligence, is absolute. Thus, efforts to conceal must be doubled when there is any possibility that the uncertainty is visible.

The same absolutism often characterizes both work and family life. To appear unequivocal is the mark of our *machismo*. It is the strength we admire and we go to great lengths to pretend to possess it. This is why Fromm could say, "Our social pattern is such that the successful man is not supposed to be afraid or bored or lonely." What an incredible burden to put on anybody: to be above very ordinary, universal human traits! What an assured formula for generating concealment. But the deception is endlessly fragile. It only has to be shown that such success is guilty of human frailty for one's mask to be removed. Is it any surprise that by the time of mid-life, having sustained the pretenses for years, a person is either completely broken to saddle and will docilely pace as required until retirement, or is tempted to dramatically overthrow all of one's past. By any criterion of leadership, which of these people is qualified to lead? Surely not the shuffling pretender, such is the tragedy of Willy Loman; and not the person who must destroy everything. The former represents the weakness of impotence, the latter the weakness of violence. The former would be unable to recognize evil in the rise of Nazism; the latter would destroy a village in order to save it. The potential for mature life and leadership surely is to be seen in the "weakness" of the person intentionally struggling with the traumas of mid-life. Sufficiently in touch with one's fear, boredom and loneliness, such a person will discover that, while real, these are demons whose power derives from our need to deny them. When embraced, our weaknesses do not destroy us; they humanize as roles never can. It is not the human condition, either at fifteen or fifty, to be unequivocally strong as roles often require us to be. To be sometimes frightened, bored, lonely, and often ambivalent about situations does not mean that one is incapable either of choosing or of recognizing the wisdom of another's decisions. After all, the process of deciding always involves some arbitrariness.

The facts never speak with such a single voice that only one course of action is possible. Value-judgements are involved in every decision and, if they are real values and not an ideology pretending otherwise, they make one capable of apparent inconsistency. A genuine conviction no more predetermines a policy than does a set of facts. A conviction which influences, without determining, a decision makes it possible to see facts in a fresh light. We had an illustration of this in a college's recent struggle over the issue of South African investments. The most radical students saw things unequivocally: Divest now! Some trustees were comparably unequivocal: Never sell investments which yield richly. After lengthy deliberations, during which the inherently moral nature of a liberal arts college was made explicit, the trustees voted a policy of selective divestiture. Determined not to dump its South African holdings en masse, thereby possibly jeopardizing their fiduciary trust, they decided to negotiate with American-based companies in the hope of persuading them to more creative social roles. If these efforts met with company resistance or indifference the trustees would be free to sell. In response to the facts of monstrous racial injustice their commitment to maximize return on investments was modified. Their commitment to social justice overrode the traditional understanding of their roles. Ideologists of whatever stripe would never be capable of this action. Such flexibility, which has moved beyond the need to pretend strength, is the

material of leadership.   By being in touch with one's own
frailties and real strengths one can be reached by new facts. That
is the stance towards which mid-life would have us move. Oscar
Hammerstein put the mid-life bewilderment simply:

> When I was a boy
> World was better spot;
> What was so, was so
> What was not, was not.
>
> Now I am a Man
> World have changed a lot:
> Some things nearly so,
> Others nearly not![9]

Looking to Erikson and Lynch again, we find that adulthood
must be understood primarily as a creative tolerance for
ambiguity. Erikson wrote, "Although aware of the relativity of
all the various life styles . . . the person of integrity knows that
for him all human integrity stands and falls with the one style of
integrity of which one partakes." Lynch, in describing ambivalence, concluded, "I can choose more freely knowing well that
another's contrary choice might be as good as my own." For
neither man does strength need to pretend the absence of
uncertainty. Doubt and relativity need neither be concealed nor
evicted; they are inherent in human experience. It is only the
inability to acknowledge uncertainties which impels us to
destroy them. It is the ability to enhance ourselves by being
human in our own distinctive way, rather than the need to
conform to roles or to require others to do so, which is the mark
of adulthood. It is this ability which many adolescents who
conformed too completely to roles are seeking at mid-life.

Two other realities of the middle years must be noted. First,
few attitudes prevalent in our society are more harmful than our
refusal to admit the inseparability of gains and losses. Despite
the contrary evidence from experience we continue to assume
that, over the course of our development, losses should be
avoidable. There is, of course, the important sense in which we
should be able to accumulate insights and self-understandings
to which we come through our experience. As we know,

however, even these gains are elusive. We have them only to the extent that we are able to incorporate them into the way we relate to ourselves and to others. In successful internalization of such gains we gradually become unaware of them. They have become part of who we are.

But, not only are such gains more difficult to sustain than we ordinarily admit, they are also always accompanied by comparable losses. At those times of our various graduations— out of diapers; into a bed from a crib; kindergarten, schools; into adolescence; into marriage; into parenthood; into frailty—we both gain and lose some things. Without minimizing the gains, since they are what the claims of living require, we need to acknowledge and to make provision for the losses which always accompany them. Who has completely forgotten the sense of loss when one was moved from the outgrown crib to the hopelessly large bed? That it was a graduation and that one would grow to fit it most knew, but neither of these could obscure the reality of the loss. Later graduations involved the same, largely unacknowledged, dynamics. While most seniors are ready, even eager, to get out of high school or college, the fact is that there are poignant losses at such times. Some evidence for this assertion is to be seen in research which demonstrates that most people's memory of their high school years is more complete than for comparable periods of life.[10] Similarly, to be married, however keenly desired, clearly involves the loss of one's status as a single person. So important is the fact of our apartness, and so powerful the desire in marriage to overcome it, that I find Gibran's advice, in *The Prophet*, for an enduring marriage to be sound.

> *And stand together yet not too near together*
> *For the pillars of the temple stand apart,*
> *And the oak tree and the cypress grow not in*
>   *each other's shadow.*

Further illustrations abound: the couple who gladly welcome their first child have both gained and lost something; the divorced person, however eager to escape an intolerable relationship, both gains and loses.

We may assume that, inseparable from hard-won gains, there will be mid-life losses. I shall shortly speak of one of these but let me state here my conviction that we need to make provision over the course of lives for the experience of the grief which accompanies such loss. Throughout the life-stages there are repeated experiences of death and re-birth. Properly embraced, these are both necessary to the completion of the transitions and are potentially instructive regarding our own physical death.

The second reality which may characterize the trauma of mid-life illustrates what we have been saying about gains and losses. Given the ability of our society to have us believe that what we desire is external accumulations, that we will be happier as we possess the visible evidences of achievement, mid-life is a process of becoming clearer in our own minds as to what we do and don't desire. But it is much easier to state the process than it is to embody it. It was early in our lives that we began to recognize the importance of possessions to others and to enjoy possessing things ourselves. We bought into the system so thoroughly that whatever it praised we wanted. The list of such wants is endless. Today's television ads for any hour will identify what they are this week. The result of such externalized lives is that whatever we really want becomes ever more difficult to identify.

What may gradually dawn on us is that we don't want more of the same. Not only do the efforts required to possess ever more become tedious but the things themselves become progressively unsatisfying. Both the instrumental attitude towards one's work and the trivial things which that work enables one to purchase begin to be called into question. The quantitative formula is a problem less because it leaves so much to be desired than because of what it leaves out. And what is left out is the heart of our humanity, our internal life, our values, our genuine desires. What is gradually dropped from what David Riesman called "other-directed" lives is any capacity for self-directedness. Gone is the personal center of judgement which informs self-direction. Not only do we not know what we want until somebody dangles one of them before our glazed eyes but we do not know what we feel or think until one of the weekly newsmagazines instructs us.

It is probably not intellectually that most people first become aware that something is wrong. It is usually by some much less discussable experience: a sharp pain in the chest; the marriage (or even the serious dating) of a favorite child; the failure to receive an overdue promotion; the realization that you consumed a quart of booze over a short weekend; the death of one's parents; the onset of menopause; the realization that one has begun to think in terms of time left rather than time lived. The awareness may have less dramatic, less perceptible beginnings: loss of interest in one's job, later recognizable in progressive tolerance for shoddiness; an increase of excuses to cover one's absences from league bowling; quiet resentment of the time, as well as the money, required to maintain a suburban home; some indifference to one's personal appearance; resistance to the obligation to reciprocate entertainment; inability to imagine other ways to spend evenings than in front of television; progressive neglect of one's sexual life. The first type of experience is frightening but has the capacity to arouse; the latter, which is more common, is more dangerous because the symptoms are more gradual. The subtle process may never reach the point where it becomes possible to recognize that something has long been wrong.

The mid-life person to whom this awareness comes, whether dramatically or by the accumulation of minor clues, has several related tasks: to become clearer about those things that do matter and those that do not, and to become increasingly intentional about the former. Since time is not limitless it is important to maximize the time and energy one has for whatever is important and to minimize, where one cannot eliminate, the time spent at all else. If this counsels selfishness it is the risk that must be taken by those whose commitment to the system resulted in great self-neglect. I worry less about the selfishness of those at mid-life who are increasingly in touch with themselves than I do about the selflessness of those who are progressively self-neglecting. To be in touch with one's real desires is to be put in touch with others from the center of one's life. Clearly, I assume that the capacity for empathy arises from being in touch with one's distinctiveness, and that the ability to identify with others depends upon self-acquaintance. When no mutuality from the center of your life to another's center is possible, then only despair is left.

The mid-life opportunity for progressive intentionality involves both the embrace of one's past and the surprise gift of hope. It is from the willingness to be accountable for what has been, to acknowledge the benefits and the limitations, that the sense of a possible future comes. Thus, to evaluate prior decisions there must be careful recollection of one's youthful vulnerability; of the external lures which enabled us both to escape that vulnerability and to begin to receive the system's rewards; of the certainty we had or pretended to have; of the work satisfactions and the compulsion by which we tried both to establish our worth and to conceal our lack of a sense of it; of the meaningfulness of a few significant friendships and of the banality or manipulativeness of our externalized relationships; of the energy we sometimes drew upon for purposeful effort, and of the fatigue which resulted from our compulsive busyness and concealment. Such self-clarification is an admission of the ambivalence in our lives, our riches and our emptiness, and of our growing desire for a center from which to live more intentionally. It is the willingness to be more honest and accountable for what has been which is the key to our ability to affirm the present and to have a believable sense of a future. To combine memory and hope—not distinctive to mid-life but markedly heightened at this point by the possibility that it is one's last chance to come alive—is the mid-life task.

At least three obstacles threaten the process: the fact that it involves losses, that most of us have relatively limited experience of being honest with ourselves, and that it will be endlessly tempting to blame society for the insufficiency of our lives. Since we have already spoken about the first, and since only a progressive personal honesty will carry us into a more rewarding future, we can set these two aside and make some concluding observations about the relationship of individual lives to society.

Two things mentioned earlier may now be related. First, that societies derive their distinctive dynamics by what they emphasize and what they play down; second, that in fashioning an adolescent identity it is neither necessary nor possible to produce a wholly new self. Like all societies, ours has its ways of luring young people beyond immobilization. That we do this by emphasizing the importance of schooling, accreditation, and jobs is not in itself to be denigrated. We enjoy many privileges which result from these emphases. Developmentally, however, problems arise from two facts: youth's understandable tendency to overcommit to those achievements which society values; and that an affluent society has many rewards for the diligent and fortunate. The combination of overcommitment and the affluence to which it often leads suggests that one may ignore with impunity aspects of one's inner life, of one's relationships with others, of the values by which one's choices are informed. As mentioned before, the need for some such set of illusions proffered to the young cannot be denied. It is simply not possible to think one's way out of the impasse of contemporary relativism without some arbitrary commitments. However, the eventual consequences of our particular set of mobilizing illusions, which give mid-life its particular character in this society, cannot be ignored. What is overlooked in our emphasis on schooling, work, promotions is too important to our humanity to be endlessly neglected. Sigmund Freud, who may well have qualified as a workaholic, was wiser than most middle-class Americans at least in his recognition that satisfaction in both work and love were requisite to human well-being. It is the no longer repressible desire for this human well-being that triggers the mid-life crisis. The crisis involves the recognition that there are too many long neglected aspects of one's self. There has been for too long an imbalance in the things to which one has paid attention. It may be tempting to blame society for the fact that one is not fulfilled. But the responsibility for having chosen a life that promised success rather than fulfillment, or at least minimized the importance of the latter, must be accepted by the troubled person in mid-life. The society may have lured us but so has every society in its own distinctive ways. That there was no recognized alternative removes but part of the responsibility from the assenting individual.

It is not necessary in the mid-life yearning for fulfillment to denigrate the pleasures which came with success. Certainly it was true during adolescence, and remained the case long thereafter, that we needed the approval of others. But at that time success was the only goal we were able to pursue. Only on the basis of what Erikson calls negative identity formation could a young person deviate from the socially prescribed norms. And, as the fate of most of the collectives of the '60's indicated, even such negative identity formation needed the approval and support of others. The need for others' approval, especially when one is young, is universal.

It seems to be impossible to keep in healthy balance, and in mutually stimulating relationship, the many components of an ordinary human life. The difficulty can be seen in the successful politics of a free society in which spokespersons for the various components must find compromises which fully satisfy nobody. At another time, as the political balance shifts, the compromise will be differently made and, again, to no group's total satisfaction. At one period of a life a certain imbalance prevails, to be replaced by an imbalance which corrects some of the inadequacies of the first and will in turn require correction.

The problem in middle class America is that there is too much agreement about the desirable imbalance. We are too clearly of one mind about success and the means by which it is gained. Recognition of the inadequacies of the middle class imbalance is the trauma of mid-life. For some it calls for reacquaintance with the long-ignored adolescent within. Who, after twenty-five years of hardheaded prudence and practicality, doesn't yearn to have aroused again one's capacity for childhood wonder or adolescent dreaming? For others who have been long tucked into restrictive roles—such as women being homemakers only or men as ruthless profiteers—it may be the opportunity to get back in touch with their sexuality. For couples who grew apart while being endlessly conscientious parents, seeing to it that their children lacked no opportunity, it may be the desire to rediscover the affection and respect which first drew them together. Yet others, whose parents may long be dead, realize that they are the clan elders and wish to be free to act their age. For most, whatever their specific imbalance, it is the desire after years of meriting rewards simply to be wanted for, and to be comfortable being, nothing but oneself.

Thus understood, mid-life is a precious opportunity to gather together the disparate elements of one's life for a kind of fresh start. It will not be absolutely new; too many of the cards have been dealt. But it may be fresh at least in the important sense that one has the chance to take one's own attitude towards what has been and recognize what has really mattered and what has been pretend. Taking responsibility for one's past and accepting how one has played one's cards, is the basis for future hope. To admit what has been stressed and what has been neglected will surely influence one's future. But the determination of that future will be much more a matter of one's personal responsibility. In this lies a potential satisfaction which was, by definition, excluded from the other-directed life. It is to opt for fulfillment rather than success. While it may never be possible fully to escape the judgments of others, whether or not one feels fulfilled is known only from within. It is away from the pursuit of success that the person in mid-life often wishes to move.

If children are to survive they must learn to cross busy streets. Learning to look both ways and to act on the basis of what we see is analogous to the mid-life experience. The opportunity of mid-life is both to acknowledge the continuities of our lives and to refuse to let the past wholly determine the future. That the method by which we accomplish this involves both promise and risk completes the analogy. The temptation to hold back will be at least as strong at mid-life as it was in childhood. How confined our future will be is as real an issue now as it was then.

CHAPTER 3

Work and Human Development at Mid-life

The title of this chapter suggests, without identifying, a relationship between two central aspects of human experience. The choice of the conjunction is intentional. By it I acknowledge both my hope that they are relatable and my awareness of the difficulty of so doing. Had I chosen any of several prepositions I might have given clearer leads, for instance, Work in Human Development or Work for Human Development. On the other hand, by the choice of a verb I would have suggested the relationship affirmed by many Americans: Work Is Human Development. However, I want for now to keep the title's imprecision and implied question: How is the relationship between work and human development to be understood?

Many factors underlie my thoughts about work. Over the past forty years I've had a variety of jobs beginning with a seventh grade stint at the Verne Inn at the rate of 25¢ per hour, and proceeding through my recent efforts to complete this book. Add to this direct work experience a host of indirect observations, such as my family's attitude toward work, the work habits of friends and colleagues, research in the monumental literature about work from Perkins and Baxter in the 17th century to Studs

Terkel's *Working*, and you will begin to see why I consider work important. Freud said that work and love were the two necessities of life, that they were the only reliable guardians of sanity. (He did not mention, perhaps because he knew his own priorities, that the two necessities often make trouble for each other, to say nothing of their respective power to claim our total allegiance.)

One thing has been vexing throughout much of my work experience and that is that people expect of themselves, and of others, a wholeheartedness which is unwarranted. I used to think this was because I was a minister; I now realize that the expectation is not so limited. The ethos of most colleges is heavily influenced by the expectation, brought by students and reinforced by the place, that they will be single-minded about their work. The expectation is further empowered, at least temporarily, by our myth that hard work assures success. That it is impossible to deviate from the myths of one's community— the non-believer simply no longer belongs—creates at least two problems: it makes it difficult to reflect on what we *really* want from our lives; and it forces many to pretend a wholeheartedness that they lack. Sustained pretense may not be the deadliest of sins but it certainly is one of the most tiring. (Are student sleeping habits—too much during the term and too little at the end—a quiet protest against an unacknowledged ambivalence about work?)

With passive students at a work-oriented college the evidence of their love/hate attitudes toward education is usually indirect and muted. Late papers, incomplete assignments, and so forth, are often the tactics of passive aggression. Several years ago at a performance by the Dudley Riggs' Company, "Who Will Buy the Bicentennial?," the evidence was direct and massive. (Over the years I find public events, especially plays and films, to be occasions at which real student attitudes are often inadvertently revealed.) I refer to an act depicting a suburban second grade class. The audience clearly enjoyed the show-and-tell up to the point where the teacher turned on one of the pupils. I was not prepared for the hooting and cat-calls directed at the teacher who said, "You have failed the last ten spelling tests. How *do* you think you'll ever get into college? Don't you realize that your report card will follow you for the rest of your life?" For the most part we conceal our ambivalent feelings better than that. The unfamiliar observer would conclude that we are hard-working because we love it. We are good pretenders.

I often wonder why we are so secretive about our negative feelings about work. Do we, as some suggest, work so hard to ward off the threat of meaninglessness? Having recognized the threat are we impelled to hard work as a device to obscure it? Or, is it the case with us, as I suspect it was with Freud, that hard work is the perfect excuse for not having to deal with love? Aware of the endless demands, but less aware of the endless rewards of personal relationships, do we opt for sustained manipulative work rather than relational effort? Are we determined to retain our sanity exclusively by hard work? If so, are we aware of the perils of overburdening even such a good thing as work with excessive expectations?

Whatever the personal factors which make it difficult for us to acknowledge our ambivalence about work, we mustn't overlook the importance of community attitudes. The college and town where I live have little tolerance for anything less than wholeheartedness. By coming to college one becomes part of a community which, with much of America, has made a religion of work. The question to be asked is whether or not there is any other community to which one belongs which, without making an enemy of work, might make one capable of resisting work-idolatry. Having identified some of the perils of the religion of work let's consider briefly what the work of religion is that might help us to be responsible about our jobs without compulsively hiding behind them.

It may surprise you to learn that motivating people to work is not the work of religion. I suspect that most people, perhaps unconsciously, would say from their experience that one of the important functions of the church was to reinforce work-motivation. That is one of the unfortunate alliances made by much of Protestantism, beginning as early as the late 16th century. In order to get at the Biblical attitude toward work, however, we must first recognize that work is not inherently evil. Evidence from the Bible in such places as Genesis 2 and Psalm 104, indicates that ancient Jews had a positive attitude toward work.

Work was not their religion but at least two things must be noted about it. First, as Genesis 2 indicates, Adam worked because it was necessary. Second, in addition to providing for one's own needs, work was the most direct and regular means for serving one's neighbor. This is clearly indicated in one of the classical statements about vocation from the seventeenth century: "The first . . . thing to be intended in the choice of a trade or calling . . . is the service of God, and the public good; and therefore . . . that calling which most conduceth to the public good is to be preferred. . . ." [1]

The Bible often speaks of God as worker. The Creator is described anthropomorphically in the opening chapter of Genesis as one who worked six days in fashioning the universe. Jesus put it succinctly: "My Father worketh hither to and I work." (John 5:17) This language, though it is repugnant to other religious and philosophical traditions, has dignified virtually all useful forms of human work. This positive attitude is not, however, the only Biblical attitude toward work. More familiar, I suspect, is the characterization of work in Genesis 3:17 as one aspect of God's condemnation of Adam.

> Cursed is the ground because of you;
> In toil you shall spend all the days of your life;
> In the sweat of your face
> You shall eat bread
> Till you return to the ground,
> For out of it you were taken;
> You are dust,
> And to dust you shall return.

There are many reasons why this report of work-as-condemnation is more memorable than the irenic report in Genesis 2. Among these it may well be that work as a curse is truer to most people's experience. That is not because work is inherently evil; its potential for good under God has already been established. Rather, like all other important human activities, work has the capacity to tyrannize. Workaholism is only a contemporary way to describe lives over-committed to work's potential for giving meaning. The institution of Sabbath is a recognition of human need for a virtually absolute law prohibiting work-exploitation of others and of one's self. For most of us there is no comparable resource by which to limit the claims of endless work. When we are both not working and sober we feel guilt. This is a sophisticated bondage. Whether or not an understanding of human development might liberate us from such imprisonment is the question to which we now turn.

Reflections on human development are at least as ancient as those on work. Biblical and classical writers have pondered the progress of lives from infancy to death. Shakespeare identified seven stages: from the infant, ". . . mewling and puking in the nurse's arms," to the

> . . . last scene of all,
> That ends this strange eventful history,
> Is second childishness and near oblivion,
> Sans teeth, sans eyes, sans taste, sans everything.[2]

Alexander Pope has a comparably cynical schematization, and from an unknown French source there is a sexist caricature of the decades through which women pass which concludes with these words:

> A 60 ans elle est comme la Siberie,
> Chacun sait où elle est
> Mais . . . personne ne veut y aller.

Hinduism is predicated on four stages of life through which all men are expected to pass and recently I discovered a California scheme in which five transitional tasks within adulthood are identified.

Since there are many models to describe the stages through which lives pass between the cradle and the grave, I want to use Erik Erikson's characterizations of what he believes to be the eight stages of normal human development. In order to get at these we need first to note several important assumptions. Some of these apply to all schemes; the last three are specific to Erikson's understanding.

The first assumption is that the cycle of development through which lives pass is universal. Whether recognized or not, all persons move from birth through similar, if not identical, stages, coping as best as they are able with the continuing need for growth and development. Secondly, the particular struggles of the life-cycle are primarily internal. While there are always relevant external factors such as the character of significant persons and the characteristics of the time and place into which one is born, the life-agenda unfolds on its own timetable and is dealt with knowingly or otherwise. This emphasis on internality may be unfamiliar. More difficult yet is the fact that it is internal feelings rather than thought to which I refer. Thirdly, the life stages involve one in endless tensions arising from the need for both continuity and change. This tension is often experienced most vividly in both adolescence and mid-life, the latter being something of a recurrence of the former. But at virtually all times of our lives there is a painful and potentially creative tension between habit and the desire for novelty. Fourthly, nobody proceeds flawlessly through the life stages. While people obviously vary widely in their ability to deal with stressful situations, the fact is that all have their difficulties and these are probably more similar than we acknowledge. Finally, nobody is beyond the possibility of further growth. No living person ever reaches a stage where further development is inappropriate. Though there is legitimate resting and there are normal arrested times, all need and wish to keep growing.

The following items seem central to Erikson's schematization. I stress them both because he does not and because they seem to be crucial. First, the polar tensions at every stage are complementary rather than mutually exclusive. While at each stage the positive pole must predominate for healthy growth, the complementary pole persists appropriately in a minor role. Thus, trust must be fashioned in infancy as the primary response to reality but some mistrust is both unavoidable and functional. Second, gains and losses are cumulative. It is with the resources acquired at any given stage that one copes with the demands and opportunities of the next. What you didn't acquire you can't use. This cumulative nature of gains and losses is aggravated in a society like ours where, in the interest of early career decisions, an either/or attitude is taken toward the polar tensions found at each stage. Finally, the stages may indeed be handled out of order but always at greater cost than otherwise would have been necessary. Erikson's stages are generally chronological but age alone is no assurance of maturity. This may be the most liberating and frightening concomitant of Erikson's discoveries. A mandatory surcharge for belated attention to an issue may not be unique to personal growth but the fact of it should not be overlooked. Though costs for repair work are one thing, belated new construction of a bridge permitting deeper intimacy may, at the time, seem prohibitively expensive.

We shall examine in greater detail later this matter of the additional costs of maturation which occurs out of phase. There simply are times of life when a given development is scheduled to occur. This often involves simultaneous biological and social factors, as in the post-puberty work of fashioning a viable identity as an emerging adult. While such development is never painless there is both less trauma and some public support when it occurs at the appropriate time. The fifteen-year-old may reasonably expect more sympathy in coping with the issues of adolescence than many a person twice that age who is belatedly addressing the same questions. It results in a lack of compassion for those who are out of phase. Still, we do expect a certain growth to occur within an understood time frame.

Over the course of Erikson's understanding of human development there are polarities which are the agenda for each particular life-stage. At the outset the tension is between trust and mistrust; at the last between ego integrity and despair. While the healthy life cycle calls for dominance of the positive poles,(trust to integrity) the complementary pole is never thoroughly eliminated. It is important to repeat this for two reasons: both because it is alien to our ordinary way of efficient thinking, and, because the negative pole is often functional when allowed a subordinate role. Thus, mistrust, which becomes paranoia when dominant, is a needed resource in a world which both is and is not trustworthy.

For Erikson the initial identity crisis arises in terms of trust and mistrust. The quality of relationship between the mothering person and the infant is decisive for the development of the sense of harmony or disharmony between the self and the world. In his words, basic trust is ". . . an attitude towards one's self and the world derived from the experiences of the first year." [3] I understand this to mean that the experience of the world as primarily trustworthy leads to a sense of trust in one's self, which is to say, trust in one's perceptions of reality.

His next three stages are traversed during the pre-school years. Corresponding roughly to Freud's anal, genital, and latency stages, they represent the development of will, initiative, and a sense of competence. The achievement of a sense of autonomy rather than shame and doubt, which is the second task and occurs primarily in connection with bowel control, represents the ability to balance self-expression with self-control. Failure to achieve such self-mastery yields a continuing, crippling sense of shame. Such a personality ". . . would like to destroy the eyes of the world. Instead he must wish for his own invisibility." [4] The third task calls for the development of a sense of initiative. Here the autonomous capacity for self-expression must learn to use that ability with and for others. Here is the beginning of conscience, for the child's growth potential must be moderated by the parents' way of living. Here also are the roots of all later male and female initiatives. Failure to balance the claims of self and others results either in sociopathology, where initiative runs wild, or in the guilt of the scrupulous conscience. Scrupulosity produces men and women whose sense of worth lies only in what they can do rather than what they are as persons. The fourth task, the achievement of a sense of industry, calls for the development of an initial discrimination between work and play coupled with a sense of one's ability to make things reasonably well. Failure to develop such confidence in one's abilities results in a sense of inferiority. From this felt inadequacy the child may attempt to substitute mediocrity for a sense of meaningful industry. Alternatively, the threat of mediocrity may cause us to pour ourselves into work in a desperate effort to conceal the felt inferiority.

Stage five represents the task of adolescence and involves language for which Erikson is best known. During these years one must form an adequate identity. Failure to do so results in identity diffusion. An acceptable sense of one's self must emerge from the traumas of adolescence for the young person to be able to move on. As we shall see later, however, there is more to any young person than can completely fit into any identity formed in these years. Especially because of middle-class America's emphasis upon career and family, much of the self that is vocationally or maritally marginal gets suppressed. The onset of puberty, with its real and imagined new powers, coupled with the almost inevitable loss of childhood certainties, makes for deep instability. With everything seemingly in flux the question of one's identity is inevitable. No longer a child and not yet an adult, the question takes this form: What, if any, correspondence is there between others' estimation of me and my self-estimate? Some similarity in these estimations indicate continuity between the past and future self. Lack of such correspondence means both role diffusion and the inability to make those commitments which are the business of the next stage of one's developing life.

The more I reflect on Erikson's scheme the more I am persuaded of the great importance of his sixth stage. Whereas his language about intimacy is clear and simple, the significance and/or the difficulty of the task he describes is often covert. Intimacy is the ability to commit oneself to concrete affiliations. He does not make clear that this is the stage of life where youthful idealism must give way to the possibility of meaningful commitments to imperfection. Derived from a viable ego-identity, it is the ability to offer and to receive the offer of intimacy from another which makes such commitments to imperfection possible. Inability to make such commitments results in self-isolation and reveals some fear of imperfection. In a perfect world there would only be tasks which could be carried out flawlessly. In the present world there are only imperfect tasks imperfectly executed. The isolated person declines all tasks in which s/he is not fully assured of success for only such tasks assure that no loss to the self will result. Only intimacy empowers us to attempt tasks that have uncertain outcomes. Intimacy permits commitment; isolation precludes it.

The polar tensions at Erikson's seventh stage involve generativity and stagnation. Generativity is not to be equated with the fact of physical parenting. A marriage of genuine mutuality includes the desire to combine ". . . personality and energies in the production and care of common offspring." [5] But

Erikson's understanding of generativity is much broader than this. It involves a concern for the future society, a caring relationship to all youth.

To the extent that generativity was an ingredient, however unconscious, in a teacher's choice of his/her vocation, it both shapes those relationships and involves a special risk. Whereas stagnation calls for patterns of dependency—we hear professors speak of "my students" or of protégés—generativity seeks to nurture independence and initiative. The generative relationship seeks to assure students that they have the potential for becoming at least as capable as their teachers. A risk, as we saw in the 1960's, is that a given generation of youth may reject the ways in which elders offer friendship.

Erikson's understanding of the final stage of the life cycle involves the polarities of integrity and despair. The achievement of integrity involves at least the following: the mature person accepts his/her life story as the only one possible for him/her; is lovingly free from the wish that his/her parents had been different; accepts full responsibility for his/her life; feels kinship with people of other times and places who created things of value; and is prepared to defend his/her life-style against external threats. An integrated adult is able both to lead and to follow as appropriate.

These are Erikson's eight normal stages through which all people proceed well or ill. They are metaphors of human development. On the pilgrimage from birth to death they help to identify the unavoidable antinomies at the times of transition. How we handle each of these determines our ability to move onto the next developmental task. Failure to achieve whatever is normal for any given stage contributes to some unhealthy adaptation at the next. All people fail in varying degrees.

Having found Erikson's descriptions of the life stages helpful in interpreting my own experience, I should note a problem which some people have when it comes to applying his generalizations to their particular experience. The fact is that I first discovered his material in the course of mid-life. At that stage I was less concerned with the distinctiveness of my own experience than with the extent to which that experience fell within the range of normalcy. Often unsure of their distinctiveness, or unable to claim responsibility for their lives to date, many young people resent Erikson's apparent claim that their experience is necessarily much like that of all others of comparable age. In one sense this is a difficult assertion to acknowledge; in another one of those beautiful truths which age may be best able to affirm.

We are now able to speak about the relationship of work to human development. Let me be as clear as possible about my attitude towards work: it is an important activity for most people during an important period of their lives. For healthy adults it is desirable both as a primary outlet for energies and creativity and as the principal means by which to serve society. Through work we may serve both ourselves and the world.

But it is with reference to the demands of the life-cycle that work must also be viewed. Though work is necessary for the maintenance of life, it is often misused in two ways: as an end in itself and as a means of concealing our neglect of equally basic human activity. It is not the criterion by which all of the life stages are to be judged. Both childhood and aging, for example, involve personal developments to which work may be inimical. And if we recognize that the child and the elder are characters at all of life's stages, characters in need of lines despite the minor parts allowed them during the adult years, we see why work must not be allowed to dominate all other activities. The extent to which either play (an activity of one's continuing childhood) or meditation (an activity of maturity) is regularly justified for its eventual work-enhancement reveals such domination.

Work is an important, often necessary, human activity and the human task is to be able to affirm it responsibly. The dangers are the old ones of either work-compulsion or sloth. I suspect that, despite their seemingly antithetical traits, both of these extremes have in common a rejection of the demands of human development. That work compulsion often serves both the personal and the societal desire to restrain other aspects of living has been clearly stated by a contemporary psychoanalyst, Allen Wheelis.

> . . . Work strengthens conscience; leisure facilitates impulse.
> . . . Work, therefore, has been considered a necessary aid to the

superego in its task of curbing sexual and aggressive impulses. . . .
Painful labor is both punishment for past sin and insurance
against further sinning. Work is best able to implement the
control of impulse if it is difficult and continuous. . . . To the
extent that work has become easy and leisure has increased,
the superego has been deprived of support in its function of
repression.[6]

The problem with work obligations, especially in our society,
is that for many people they are very difficult to restrain. Largely
gone are the resources of the Sabbath and of the Protestant Work
Ethic which, for similar reasons, set limits to work. That
Sabbath-observance was intended to do this may be less
surprising than the fact that Calvin agreed. While there is a
political and social conservatism in his *The Institutes of the
Christian Religion*, there is also recognition of the perils
inherent in unbridled human ambition. Today the former may
be unacceptable; the latter we urgently need. It was those who
". . . may sometimes, perhaps, achieve something apparently
laudable. . ." that Calvin's understanding of vocation sought to
protect against their own "rashness." Coupled with the more
familiar encouragements to hard work were correlative re-
straints for him who ". . . will be impelled by his own temerity to
attempt more than is compatible with his calling. . . ." [7] The
work ethic sought both to dignify and to set limits to worldly
work. It has been our failure in the latter which has increasingly
troubled us for the past two centuries.

It is my judgement that the work ethic, which was not a
foolproof guard against avarice (is such possible?), went awry
when it lost its religious foundation. The abandonment of the
theological basis for work-responsibility is seen most clearly in
the writings and enduring influence of Benjamin Franklin. In the
Sage of Philadelphia and his successors we find prudence
substituted for piety, self-interest for social responsibility, moral
exhortation for fear of God. It may be no easier today to draw
upon the resources of the Reformers than upon those of the
Lord's Day but we need at least to recognize our consequent
vulnerability to work's unending demands.

With reference to the absolutizing tendency inherent in work, the task is to discover a basis on which one may affirm work responsibly but not compulsively. The temptations are either to idolize or to despise it, to believe either that nothing is more important or that anything is permissible which enables one to avoid work. Neither extreme is personally acceptable since both have excluded that freedom which is intrinsic to our humanity. All compulsive behavior is undesirable because, by suppressing realities which are germane to the issue at hand, it refuses real decision. A free person is one who occasionally has the choice to work or to decline it. Many students have a hard time with this, which may be why there is so much grimness and so little joy amidst all the busyness. I have observed little change in these patterns during a quarter century at a particular college, described as a place where people work hard and play hard. While partly true, this obscures the educationally, and developmentally, crucial fact that we sharply separate work and play. Serendipity always gives way to control. Reason and emotion aren't allowed to enhance and restrain each other. It may be immediately efficient to compartmentalize life like this, but I find the long range implications ominous. Either rationality will be insulated against the joys of emotion, or the individual will suffer unbridled sensuality. These are unacceptable alternatives. We are compulsive about both to the detriment of intellectual ferment and the opportunities for personal maturation. Not free to acknowledge ambivalent feelings about our work, or about much else, we either capitulate to its endless demands or try to live as though it didn't exist. In neither response is the God-given wholeness of life or the importance of the final struggle between integrity and despair acknowledged.

Our unfortunate aversion to ambivalence begins early and is compounded by the way we handle adolescence. Theologically viewed, we seem to assume that with impunity we may transfer to any object or activity the single-mindedness once reserved to God alone. While the perils of such idolatry were long ago recognized, we either do not recognize them, or worse, believe that we may flourish at what others tried to avoid.

Whether or not they actually have the symbolic power to turn us in a new direction, I find in Erikson's presentation of the life-stages a potential aid. As I indicated above, the central fact in his understanding is the polar tension at each of the stages. While the tension must be favorably resolved for one to be able to move with maximum strength to the next stage, the point is that both ingredients of the prior stage are taken along and that both are functional. This is clearly seen in those adolescent developments involving the polarities of identity-formation and identity diffusion. To be able to move from adolescence to the commitments of intimacy and of adult work one must have fashioned and had confirmed by others a credible sense of oneself. Failure to achieve some such sense of the continuity in one's life results in an inability to make those appropriate connections with others both in intimacy and at work. So, this is no argument for identity-diffusion.

But, the temptation persists to pretend clearer self-understanding than one has. And our society, for reasons which I shall not try to explicate here, encourages such pretense. We simply fail to see that, despite the accompanying inefficiency, some uncertainty about one's identity is functional. Given the richness of our lives, which results from the life-stages previously navigated, we cannot, for example, squeeze our whole selves into a narrow career box. (Something similar could be said about our commitments in intimacy. No single person can respond to all of the complexities of another but that should not be expected. The point of an adequate, though incomplete, identity is that it makes us capable of making and sustaining commitments to imperfection both in love and in work.) One may discover that many careers enable us to draw upon more of our human resources than are required to qualify for the job. Thus, some college teachers, trained for the research of graduate schools, discover that they have skills as counselors or in administration (to say nothing of faculty softball!) which were apparently irrelevant to their appointment. The point is simple: there is always more to each of us than is indicated in any identity we fashion as adolescents or young adults. Given a primarily positive sense of who we are there is room for considerable uncertainty about the rest. The capacity for tolerating internal ambivalences is a fundamental human resource. To lack such tolerance means a life of pretense which is at best fatiguing and at worst tragic. It often takes a mid-life crisis to make us recognize the extent to which we have been pretending.

I suggest that the roots of many such crises reach back at least to adolescence. During those traumatic years, when so many previous certainties disintegrate, there are powerful internal reasons for concealing one's bewilderments. When to those reasons is added external pressure to know what you're going to do with your life it is virtually impossible for the young person not to absolutize his or her decisions. Other such yearnings, or even aptitudes, that one may have get shunted aside in the pursuit of one's career. The perils resulting from the inability to admit our ambivalence are not confined to the public realm. Such inability also makes us intolerant of internal eccentricities. Rather than being stimulated and nourished by differences we try to expunge them from society and from ourselves. The older I get the more am I attracted to Emerson's observation that "A foolish consistency is the hobgoblin of little minds. . . ." In all events, the work to which adolescents give themselves, including that of the college years, often functions as a means of concealing other developmental assignments. One of the troubling features of an academically strong college is that the professed need to study is essentially unchallengeable. What is being ignored, or concealed, when any obligation, or excuse, is so universally accepted? Outside the academy the same question may be asked of those who always respond with, "We have a prior engagement," when they need an acceptable excuse for declining an unanticipated invitation. What covert assumptions sustain these practices?

There are undoubtedly many factors in mid-life which help explain the resurfacing of these issues for an increasing number of people. One factor is that mid-life is a period when people gradually begin to think in terms of time left rather than time lived. One day it dawns on everyone that s/he has lived more than half of his/her life. To illustrate the struggle which ensues let me share portions of a recent letter from a friend recovering from cardiac arrest.

> . . . one of the best things about heart attacks is their capacity to convert one's work idolatry into wholesome ambivalence. . . .

Leisure becomes not only permissible, not only legal, but a moral requirement . . . with doctors, nurses, spouse and friends insisting upon it. . . .

But there is a hook, as well as bait. . . . As my stamina increases so does my guilt about wallowing around luxuriously in that pool of sloth. What do I do about it? Right, you've guessed correctly: I work. Just a wee bit . . . scribbling about in preparation for an address and a paper down the road. It has now become a daily necessity. . . .

How are we to tell when we are so possessed by work that we are blind to its lethal potential? Does working ourselves to death reflect a sound attitude toward work? What will prompt us to consider using whatever time remains in a better fashion?

Another factor is that mid-life is a time when, having had a wide range of experiences, many yearn for a deepening rather than further broadening of their lives. Peguy observed, "Forty is a merciless age. . . . This is the time when we become who we are." [8] Since I do not share his negative evaluation of becoming who we are I would call forty a merciful age. Whatever the chronological age at which it occurs, this is the point at which one becomes able to recognize the inauthenticity of much busyness and begins to pay attention to neglected aspects of one's life. It is a time for distinguishing between one's pretenses and those things about which we can be intentional. This is the beginning of a process of simplification which culminates in the beauty of older people whose lives are centered rather than cluttered. Gradually freed from clock-bound and task-determined living, such elders take necessary time for the life-giving seasons and processes. In Erikson's language they achieve integrity rather than despair. They are able to affirm their lives rather than be disgusted by a retrospective view.

Finally, mid-life may be the time for progressive honesty in one's self-appraisal. Gone, or going, is the need for fantasies. One's achievements, however incomplete, constitute the sufficiently firm basis of one's self-understanding. Gone, or going, is the dependence on roles. One's own story, with all of its oddities and embarrassments, becomes the increasingly clear source out of which one lives. Motivation comes less from other's expectations of me than from my own needs, real resources, and desire to relate to others from my own center. Gradually it becomes clear that I may no longer decline personal responsibility. Ultimately, only I am accountable for my life. Others have, and continue to exercise, significant influence. That is inescapable, but the emphasis changes. Many relationships will and should deepen at this time. The point is that these relationships do not exhaustively define us. There is an inherent dialectic between ourselves and the outside world and it is the business of mid-life to move us beyond fantasy-filled and role-defined existence toward a more accurate awareness of who we really are and what we have to share.

That busyness may, and often does, function as a shield against encountering the life-stage questions is not, however, sufficient basis for utterly negative attitudes toward work. It is too important an activity to be rejected. As with all of the basic components of our lives, all of which at one time or another attempt takeovers, what we need are means by which to encourage and at the same time set limits for them. What these means may be is, frankly, not clear. Either they will be recovered from our religious past or discovered in some empirical understanding of the universal needs of human development.

In the meantime our work experiences may be seen as an important source for relevant questions. Needless to say, the young apprentice and the person approaching retirement neither will nor should be sensitive to the same work-derived issues. Our task is to entertain these questions and to locate other people who find themselves similarly addressed. Such collegiality is both protection against idiosyncrasy and the basis for making whatever behavioral adjustments may be appropriate.

As we become convinced that there is always more to who we are than fits any single category, always more growth of which we are capable, the developmental question remains: Is my present range of experience putting me in touch with ever more of my own exciting and frightening resources? It was this question of which I gradually became aware with the onset of my own middle years. It is to that question that we may now turn.

CHAPTER 4

Vocational Menopause: Mid-life As Plateau

I am not certain when my interest in the phenomena of mid-life began. My awareness that I was getting older—no longer a "young man with promise," if I ever was that!—began at a Sunday dinner many years ago. In the course of clearing the table our son patted the back of my head and said with all the compassion of a child: "Dad, you're getting bald."

It must have been about fifteen years ago that I became conscious that something was bothering me. It was not just the matter of aging. I had the sense somewhere around my fortieth birthday that I was arriving at a kind of plateau. After two decades of demanding growth such as learning what it meant to be married, accepting the responsibility of parenthood, clearing the various academic hurdles and learning to do a job passably, I realized that an era of my life was coming to an end. The cliff-face I'd been climbing had begun to level out.

It was not that I felt I had been a failure. The symptoms were imprecise. I didn't then recognize that I had largely completed several of the tasks which society imposes on us. I certainly did not recognize that what I really wanted to do with my life was not a question which I had asked for a long time. A variety of reasonably clear obligations had long precluded such reflections.

With one exception, to which I shall return later, I don't think the symptoms have ever become all that clear-cut. Even now I cannot state the issue more precisely than this: Am I sufficiently in touch with my own feelings to know what I want to be and to do? Assuming that such clarity is possible, am I able to act on those guidings confident that nothing is more important? Do I—can I—know myself well enough to be progressively more intentional about the way I wish to spend the balance of my life? Perhaps it would help in trying to identify these vague symptoms to recall lines from T.S. Eliot which have haunted me periodically:

> Where is the Life we have lost in living?
> Where is the wisdom we have lost in knowledge?
> Where is the knowledge we have lost in information?
> The cycles of Heaven in twenty centuries
> Bring us farther from God and nearer to the Dust.[1]

However imprecise this may be, the point I want to stress is that I am now convinced that nothing is more important than being progressively in contact with these feelings. I also think that long neglect of one's feelings directly contributes to mid-life crisis.

This stress upon the importance of one's own feelings, which may be my most important discovery in the past decade, does not fit the academic vocation well. Middle-class people generally have not been encouraged to get in touch with their own feelings and few try as hard as academicians do to substitute thought for feelings. In mid-life the academic may experience a peculiar double bind: his or her personal and professional needs may seem to be at irreconcilable odds. I shall return to this dilemma but for now let me simply report some observations which Jung made toward the end of his life.

> . . . substituting for psychic reality [is] an apparently secure, artificial, but merely two-dimensional conceptual world in which the reality of life is well covered up by so-called clear concepts. Experience is stripped of its substance, and instead mere names are substituted, which are henceforth put in the place

of reality. No one has any obligations to a concept; that is what is so agreeable about conceptuality—it promises protection from experience. The spirit does not dwell in concepts, but in deeds and in facts. Words butter no parsnips; nevertheless, this futile procedure is repeated ad infinitum.

In my experience, therefore, the most difficult as well as the most ungrateful patients, apart from habitual liars, are the so-called intellectuals. With them, one hand never knows what the other hand is doing. They cultivate a 'compartment psychology.' Anything can be settled by an intellect that is not subject to the control of feeling—and yet the intellectual still suffers from a neurosis if feeling is undeveloped.[2]

Let me go back to that plateau on which I found myself at about age forty to report one experience. Feeling uncomfortable with what had initially been the challenges of my job, I mentioned this to a senior administrator who had been very encouraging to me. A non-directive counsellor I knew he was not but I had not anticipated the intensity of his reaction. Not only was he not prepared to deal with me as a younger colleague who was experiencing some distress, but to my suggestion that anybody might be uncertain about his/her life at age forty his only response was to engender guilt in me for having such feelings. What does this man's reaction reveal about the attributes which qualify one for leadership in our society? Was my willingness to disclose my vulnerability, my uncertainties, so threatening to him that he could react only by attacking me? Must a leader only evince clear, positive views? Is unassailable self-confidence the desideratum? An ability to make timely decisions is obviously important but does apparent strength allow for the give-and-take which should precede all important decisions, to say nothing of allowing response to acknowledged weakness?[3]

Was I crazy? How could anybody as fortunate as I have any questions about his life? I had reasonably good health; had married a wonderful woman; we had children whom we enjoyed and many of whose interests we shared. I had credentials for employment at a good college and a job which I apparently performed adequately. What the hell was wrong with me?

Fortunately, I turned next to a friend who, though he couldn't understand my distress, was not judgmental. My training in counselling had impressed upon me the importance of avoiding judgments of people in need—somebody had long ago made it clear to me that "The one thing sick people don't need is advice!"—and I had tried to honor this in my own counselling. However, I never really understood the life-giving importance of nonjudgmentalism until I experienced it in the friend to whom I turned. I did not make significant progress in my conversations with this person but the important corner had been turned. I had admitted that all was not well with me and in the process had not been rebuked. My wise friend had not withdrawn from me for having ambiguous feelings about my life. I was not utterly outside of the human world. Years passed, however, before I understood that the mid-life blues which I had feared were peculiar to me were actually widespread.

During those years of uncertainty few attitudes were as unproductive as these two: the sense that my problems were idiosyncratic and, in the eyes of some, utterly unwarranted; the need in the academy to pretend strength and to conceal weaknesses. That the need for deception compounded my sense of isolation, which I now see as unnecessary, made me resentful and at the same time, made me determined to share some personal experiences and professional reflections about the mid-life crisis. My motivations for doing this are obviously numerous. In addition to those mentioned is the desire to share research which was both emotionally and cognitively motivated. The existential need for understanding persisted with varying degrees of intensity for a decade; it was only gradually that various forms of relevant material came to my attention.

Before attempting a review of some of my reading and musings in the past decade I should note the role of the work I did several years ago with a college committee on student careers. Several things became clearer in the course of that project. The first was the simple realization that, however important their problems, too much exclusive attention can be given to students' needs. This is especially true when others who are supposed to be part of the solution to such matters are themselves struggling with aspects of the problem. The second and related thing I observed was that many of the concerns of the adolescent were not confined to teenagers. I recognized that many of these questions had re-surfaced in my own life, that there was more adolescence in my maturity than I had realized and that I and others pretended confidence which we lacked. This led to a suspicion: that, for their own maturation, students might well need to know that we are reasonably viable adults despite the uncertainties of our personal and professional lives.

To the best of my knowledge a decade ago, however, nobody knew about, and certainly few were writing about symptoms of mid-life. About all that I knew was that I saw neither the accuracy nor the humor of the cliche, Life Begins at Forty. The extensive research into the dynamics of infancy and childhood was being extended by people like Erikson to adolescence and what Keniston termed "youth." Elisabeth Kübler-Ross had work under way at Billings Hospital to understand the processes of coming to terms with one's death. However, little useful material came to my attention concerning the period between adolescence and senility.

The widespread experience of the crisis inherent in the middle years is now well recognized. This is hardly information that we should have been dependent upon authorities to identify. I suppose it has something to do with the youth orientation of our society and our inability to attach worth to aging. In this, as in many things, we are unlike older civilizations, like those in India which have long recognized and found ways honorably to take account of advancing years.

At Yale an interdisciplinary study group has for several years been studying what they call "the male change of life." Involving people like Daniel Levinson, Kenneth Keniston, and Edward Klein, this group describes symptoms as follows:

> In the mid-life years, the machinery of the body may show signs of wear and aging for the first time. Changes take place, many of them of an exterior, visible sort. A man's hair grays or begins to thin. The qualities of physical attractiveness which were present in youth now dim and the evolution into middle age begins. Sexual capacity and desire may be diminished. The stairs seem longer to climb, and that occasional game of football seems more exhausting. Colds are more irritating and they linger longer. A man may suddenly realize that his co-workers think of him as middle-aged, something he himself had not begun to do.

With aging, a man must come to terms with his own mortality. From early childhood he has known intellectually that someday he will die. But conditions of the mid-life years often lend this recognition a more emotional and direct reality. He may experience anxiety and despair when friends, colleagues, and co-workers die. Death, in brief, casts a longer and darker shadow.

The mid-life years seem to require the development of a different, generally more realistic sense of who one is. It is in this period, according to Levinson, that strongly held beliefs about one's self and one's relationships with others are often seen as illusions. 'In growing up,' he says, 'everyone nurtures fantasies or illusions about what one is and what one will do.' A major task of the mid-life decade involves coming to terms with those fantasies and illusions.[4]

Martin Symonds, a training analyst at the American Institute for Psychoanalysis and Professor of Clinical Psychiatry at the New York University School of Medicine, has identified four stages through which one ordinarily passes: (1) shock and denial—the gray hairs, the expanding middle, the tired feelings are pushed away; (2) fright: this phase is usually characterized by anxious, clinging behavior; (3) the classic depression, the apathy, the "What the hell's the use?"; (4) the fourth stage ordinarily involves the resolution of the depression via some combination of a locker-room pep talk ("No more whining! Show people you're not defeated yet! No more excuses!") and a sobering, painful and liberating process of self-discovery.[5] The potential for renewal which Symonds underlines in this popular article is stressed by all who write about the subject. Nobody says renewal is necessary. Probably most people just grit their teeth and gain little from their mid-life experiences. But the potential for significant growth is rarely as heightened as in mid-life. What enables some to seize the opportunity which others reject is the question on which research is needed.

Lest any be tempted to think that these descriptions apply only to people outside the academy, let me remind you of what Nevitt Sanford has written:

It turns out that college professors develop as individuals in much the same way that other people do. Their development is progressive and is marked by distinctive stages, which are only loosely related to chronological age.[6]

Sanford identifies the stages as follows: ". . . the achievement of a sense of competence in one's discipline or specialty; self-discovery, in which the faculty gives attention to other abilities, interests, and aspirations, and so expands his personality; and discovery of others." In conclusion he notes that "As in Erikson's (1959) formulation of stages, identity is followed by intimacy and generativity. Now the professor is prepared to use all of his skills in general relationship with other people; he may find it comfortable and enjoyable to take a fatherly role with some students—those who can stand it or will accept it." Keep this description of optimal faculty development in mind for assurance when I refer shortly to a more recent article by Peter Loewenberg.

In addition to the universal fact of mid-life there are factors in our time and society which compound the problem. Put perhaps too simply they involve this question: Can I confirm basic decisions which I made much earlier in my life? This is an especially vivid question because it forces one to deal with the fact that some, if not all, of our important early decisions were made partly on the basis of ignorance and in response to cultural pressures of which we were but dimly aware.

The pressures I have in mind are partly the result of the difference between the resources required today and those people needed in times when little free choice existed. When men and women essentially relived their parent's lives, married people chosen for them by their parents, perpetuated parental values, quite different human skills were needed from those requisite today. In earlier times one needed the ability to stick with one's fate as far as work, mate, and values were concerned. That such a style of life had its own virtues must be obvious; that few things are more remote from our lives is self-evident.

With the increasing enlargement of areas of choice a person has the need for impossible skills: self-knowledge; information about the widest range of work, mates, and values; plus the ability to match properly knowledge of self and of the world. Nobody is so wise. Commitments were made, however, as though we lived in the world of our remote ancestors. Rather than recognizing that the best we were capable of under the circumstances were provisional, exploratory commitments, we acted, and were encouraged to act, as though we knew enough to be capable of utterly binding decisions.

Let me complicate this situation at least one stage further by suggesting that we were all heavily influenced in these decisions by values and goals which were much more culturally than personally determined. We have all been led to believe that the satisfactions held up to us as the rewards of certain kinds of effort would indeed satisfy us. For me, part of the task of mid-life has been to try to determine just what nourishment I do and don't derive from these socially-defined goals. On some matters I know I was misled. About others I am and may remain unclear. What I do know is that there are areas not significantly related to my own wishes in which I have made a great effort. It is those which I am trying to identify and to minimize in the balance of my life.

Whether or not that will help me to be in better touch with my own feelings is unclear. To the extent that these efforts to be reacquainted with my own inner life succeed I hope for a reinvigoration of my will. Part of the crisis of the past decade has resulted in the realization that too much of my life has been determined by an effort to force myself to certain performances for which I had little or no heart. This is a plight to which those of us in the so-called "helping professions" are easily driven. It is an irony for those who would "do good" that they often become progressively out of touch with their own wishes and have trouble locating them in a time of need.

We were ignorant when we made many of the important decisions of our youth. However, we were not completely ignorant. Some of the choices we made were near enough to being right to be confirmable in mid-life. Those which involved a mis-match have long suggested their inadequacy. It is to be hoped that courage may be found to confirm or not to confirm earlier decisions as experience has instructed us.

Of the final level of this analysis I want to speak specifically of my own vocation and two prefatory things must be said. First, it could be highly controversial. It has to do with where and how we work, about which professionals have never been known to be mute. You may not like, or even recognize, some of the things I want to stress. I may not have understood well what was happening to me. The question to which I hope some will attend however, is whether or not my experiences illumine the experiences of other teachers. Secondly, at the moment I care less about the accuracy of this particular section. Should my views be faulty I shall not be distressed, if at least one of two things, and preferably both, happen: that we gain some clarity about our life-situations and that we undertake to help each other understand better what is actually happening in our lives.

Before turning to several specific features of the academic profession which may complicate one's adjustment to mid-life, let me suggest that there are a number of ways in which we all cope with the periodic loss of interest in our disciplines, our teachings, and the hard core of our work. The easiest solution is to change jobs. For some the offer of administrative responsibility may be the opportunity for renewal. Others leave the academy and thereby bless both the place and themselves. More common is the ability to find campus responsibilities other than in one's own field. The time, energy and imagination which go into college governance, committee work, sports, and other college-related activities illustrate the latter. Too often, I fear, people simply keep to themselves any and all deep uncertainties which they have about their vocation. On every campus there is private suffering among those who must deny, even to themselves, that anything has changed. While it is still possible we all call upon our will, our sense of duty, to force us to attend to material in which we were once interested in the hope that, mysteriously, it may again yield some of its earlier satisfactions. In these, and a variety of other ways—some, like alcohol, are quite destructive—we do what we can to sustain our morale.

Regarding these matters I found another essay, "The Vocational Hazards of Psychoanalysis," by Allen Wheelis helpful. He identifies characteristics of various forms of work which may be relevant to our discussion.

> Many vocations are, in quality of experience, easily known: the nature of work in carpentry and chemistry, for example, may be

correctly perceived by those whose acquaintance with these fields is relatively slight. There are a few vocations, however, which are truly knowable only after long experience. Those which mislead belong to this group. They have a quality which cannot be fully communicated in words. One has to find out for one's self. The most painful states of inner turmoil, the severest tests of integrity, arise in those professions which have these combined characteristics: of being truly knowable only from within; and of offering promise, when viewed from without, of alleviation of inner conflict—which promise is insidiously retracted by increasing proficiency in the field. Art is one such; the church is another; and, without the implication that this completes the list, I suggest that psychoanalysis is a third.[7]

Might academic teaching be another such employment? One neither knows the work, nor its deeper rewards and stresses, until one has made an almost irreversible commitment to it. Many discover too late both its nature and their lack of affection for it.

Several years ago certain evidences suggested to me, and to a few others, that I was at such a point. I was increasingly harassed by the seemingly endless demands of the various aspects of my job. As I came to visualize this, and once verbalized to a college group, I felt that I was being devoured. I suspect that it does not take much imagination to sense that this was unhealthy imagery. Although I was unable at the time to recognize it, I resented being unable to take more time for the things I really wanted to do. Whether it was cause or effect, and the matter was then immaterial, I felt increasingly unsure of what I really wanted. You may be assuming that I choose to report these matters because they are now resolved. Hardly. I have done little more than acknowledge these tremors in my life and have just begun the endless process of becoming acquainted with their causes.

Finally, I want to identify three ingredients of the academic life which may make it difficult for us to cope with the mid-life crisis. The first, which is not unique to academics, is that we chose this work in the hope that we might thereby resolve certain inner conflicts. While this may often work as expected, it is just as often the case that inner conflicts which one had hoped the professoriate would alleviate are actually aggravated by one's professional responsibilities. Earlier I quoted Sanford to the effect that generativity—the desire to participate in the molding of the next generation—was probably one of the motivational factors in the decisions of those who enter teaching. The problem is that we both want and do not want such a relationship with the young, and we often vacillate between the poles in any given day. Events of a decade ago, in which students changed dramatically their expectations of what is acceptable and unacceptable in relationships with instructors, clearly threw many teachers off balance. There will be few Mister Chips who gracefully age in the warming admiration of their pupils.

A more obvious, and perhaps more important, characteristic of the academic profession is its preference for abstraction rather than for feelings. I trust that I will not be read as merely anti-intellectual at this point. I believe deeply in what Peter Loewenberg writes: "Intellectualization and isolation are necessary and adaptive to the mind. Data must be structured and conceptualized to be used." At the same time I am also in agreement with what he perceives as the misuses of intellect referred to in the following:

> Intellectuals have an insatiable desire to argue about abstract subjects. . . . We soon discover, however, that this fine intellectual performance makes little or no difference in actual behavior. The intellectual's comprehension of idea systems does not prevent him from being blind to what is going on inside himself and inside others. While he has eroticized thought—deriving gratification from the process of thinking, criticizing, and debating—his behavior is determined by other factors. . . .
>
> . . . Intellectualization may also be a defense against experience. Preferably the ordering and abstract intellectualization should occur after the emotional cognition. The abstract discussions in which academic intellectuals delight are often not genuine attempts at solving real problems. Their intellectualization is rather an indication of an alertness for the breakthrough of the emotional problems underneath, and their unconscious defense is to transpose into abstract thought what they do not wish to feel.[8]

Earlier in this book I suggested that mid-life may generate a peculiar double bind for the academician: one's personal need for deeper acquaintance with one's own feelings may violate the established canons of one's professional life. That some such conflict also underlies the reactions of many faculty to some of the student demands since Berkeley does not seem unlikely.

The third trait of the academic profession which may complicate our resolution of mid-life is this: we are confirming persons who are ourselves in real need of confirmation. By confirmation I mean what Buber means: ". . . the wish of every man to be confirmed as what he is, even as what he can become, by men; and the . . . capacity in man to confirm his fellow-men in this way." [9] That all people are potential confirmers and in need of confirmation I accept. That teachers are especially called upon to help youth confirm themselves seems to me equally obvious. Perhaps it is not until one approaches mid-life and the capacities for self-generating élan diminish that confirmers begin to recognize their own unmet need for confirmation. Leslie Farber, a Washington, D.C., psychiatrist, has said some things that are germane:

> . . . human nature being what it is, the man who pours out his . . . energy in confirming others will need more, and not less, confirmation of himself. . . .
>
> This makes the therapist unusually dependent on the confirmation he can get from friends and family, and especially from colleagues. . . .[10]

In this regard many of us are the victims of mistaken ideals of moral perfection. As Farber states, "Implicit in Western Society is the ideal of a teacher or healer who confirms others without needing confirmation for himself." Few assumptions are more misleading than this. We are not invulnerable towers of strength. We are merely men and women formally qualified for work that was undertaken for reasons of which we were only partly aware. To be endlessly resourceful, to have to appear strong and reliable under all circumstances, is to impose on oneself, and certainly upon others, an utterly inappropriate burden. St. Paul wisely said to those at Lystra who hailed him and his companion as gods and wanted to offer sacrifices to them, "Men, why are you doing these things? We are only human beings with feelings just like yours! . . . (Acts 14:8ff, PHILLIPS)

I do not know what hope there is that we middle-aged, who have been taught to over-value the cognitive and underrate the affective, will be able to right that balance. I find myself in agreement, however, with the views of Loewenberg.

> We need to introduce psychoanalytic education in our graduate curriculum in the social sciences. The resistance to the use of psychoanalytic theory and clinical insight among social scientists is not due to a lack of agreement among schools of depth psychology or to the difficulty of the concepts. It can be attributed to the fact that psychodynamics threatens people where they are most vulnerable. No other discipline is so immediately personal.
>
> Psychoanalysis would not only illuminate research materials; it would also have an impact on the scholar's own thoughts and feelings. It would reach to his motivations and relationships. This, of course, is highly threatening to many academics, who like nothing better than remote detachment between their work and their emotions and who will cling to this cleavage with ferocity.
>
> Christopher Jencks and David Reisman are acutely aware of the necessity of integrating subjective experience with graduate education. They say: "The critical problem of graduate instruction in the social sciences and the humanities is to narrow the gap between individual students' personal lives and their work. The graduate school must somehow put the student in closer touch with himself, instead of making him believe that the way to get ahead is to repress himself and become a passive instrument 'used' by his methods and his disciplinary colleagues. This is no mean task. The difficulty of the job is not however, an excuse for the present situation, where graduate students' subjectivity is not even regarded as a problem."[11]

Were Loewenberg to be taken seriously future generations of scholars would better navigate the waters of mid-life than some of us have done. I also suspect that they might be both better teachers and better colleagues.

CHAPTER 5

Relationships at Mid-life: Marriage

While I assume that work and love are two of the central activities of lives, we have talked more about the former. That emphasis is now to be corrected.

It would be convenient if it were possible to make the correction simply by producing material quantitatively comparable to what has been written about work. It is my suspicion, however, that there is something fundamentally misleading about dealing with work and relationships in this separate but equal way. I realize that there are many who believe strongly in such a split and I shall say some things in support of that view. To be able to affirm a relationship between one's work and one's love may be a deep desire not easily realized.

With these reservations, however, I propose to deal now with the claims of marriage at mid-life as if this relationship were largely isolatable from work. I do not assume either that marriage is the only important relationship in life or that it alone is affected by the onset of mid-life. Marriage is to a significant degree, if not absolutely in kind, a unique and important relationship. Despite the increasing incidence of divorce it is the domestic relationship of most adults. There have long been people who have chosen not to marry. For reasons arising from my ignorance, I do not intend to speak of relationships other than those of heterosexual marriage here. In the following chapter we shall look at some of the other relationships which share many qualities with married life and often enjoy a renewed importance in mid-life. In particular, I have in mind friendships and the desire to reconnect with one's family or origin.

Before launching into the topic let me clarify one issue arising from my decision to treat work and relationships separately. From my own experience I have a great deal of sympathy for one of the arguments of those who would keep them separated. They contend that one of the temptations for busy, middle-class people is for one's life at home simply to become a continuation of one's work. In many neighborhoods the loaded briefcase being carried into the house at day's end is a badge of honor. Some may sympathize with such a person but many admire and even envy one who has so many responsibilities that they cannot be completed in a normal working day. There are many reasons, some of them temporarily valid, why some people have to work evenings. I have myself done it as often as not. But, as a chronic pattern it probably signals the contamination of one area of life by another which the separationists decry. It is imperative, they say, that one be intentional about whatever the present activity is. To be at home, for example, is to be free from the obligations and constraints of the workplace and open to the obligations and constraints of the family. As one whose work has often demanded and whose family has usually tolerated a busy schedule, I know the uncertainty of being unable to distinguish clearly between work and non-work. As one whose work and family may also have benefited from my inability to keep them separated I find the absolutism of separation unacceptable. Those inclined to workaholism, or those who are deprived as the result of another's compulsion, may well insist that work contaminates all relationships and activities if not confined to the workplace.[1] To identify just who is so inclined may be just as difficult as it is to locate the incipient alcoholic. The consequences of being unable to recognize one's work-driven-ness are equally costly. Since I am now convinced that mid-life is a time of great potential for human development it may be useful to report what it was like for me. It was not opportunity but terror that I felt.

I was about forty. Nothing dramatic had occurred, nor has it since—it rarely does, but I had an inexplicable sense of uneasyness. By most criteria I was eminently fortunate. That I didn't just feel grateful, as I'd been led to believe somebody with my good fortune should, was one of the symptoms of whatever it was that had overtaken me.

I'd like to report that all this now makes sense, that I can talk about it comfortably in the past tense. That isn't true. I do have some perspective which I lacked then. I think that I better understand some of the causes of what is now referred to by some as The Wonderful Crisis of Mid-life. Such language is still too sanguine. More than anything else, I was helped out of my mid-life malaise by the gradually accelerating study and publicity which mid-life has received. Much of this is now faddish, I'm sure, but I must say that the absence of public awareness of the issues was not a help when I first encountered some of mid-life's symptoms. This fact, plus the inhospitable response of older colleagues with whom I tried to broach the issues, contributed to the guilt I felt for being "bad" or "weak," or, God help me, maybe both! The normalcy of the trauma of mid-life was, as recently as fifteen years ago, little acknowledged.

That was the word—NORMAL—which I couldn't find then. Had literature been available as it is now, to say nothing of TV programs, films, symposia, I'd have been spared considerable grief. Lacking such reassurances I read what I could, especially in the psychology of human development. I did some thinking but reflection is difficult if done alone because feelings are forever fouling ideas and ideas are never quite connecting with feelings. I needed reality checks and they were hard to find. Gradually, I began to talk publicly about what had been, and was, happening to me. During those years I never missed a day's work or, to the best of my knowledge, broke a date with my wife or children, but I was going through one of the most searching periods in my life. My appearance remained normal; but I was unable to use the same term to describe what was going on within me. It felt like I was being cut off from the human family and the isolation was painful. I did not have a communicable disease, nobody was urging quarantine, but the dis-ease which I felt was compounded by my inability to locate others who could confirm my condition. I suspect that my effort to write this book is motivated in large part by the hope that it may help some people to make their way out of an unnecessary, and not necessarily productive, isolation.

It was first within my work-life that I felt that something was wrong. I remember, some years after my difficulty began, hearing a young colleague say upon receipt of his final promotion, "My God! I'll be a Full Professor for the next thirty years!" I did understand his enthusiasm but being older I had some reservations. There comes a time—rarely as locatable as the arrival of a particular letter—when one realizes the prospect of sameness stretching out into a future which is foreseeably as long as the life one has already lived. The promotion may be valued—usually it has long been sought—but the receipt of it also sounds a kind of death knell. It represents the end of the only kind of era for which we are prepared: the era of scrambling, of getting certified, of catching somebody's eye, of demonstrating competence, of being rewarded. It is the end of the era of living by others' expectations, of looking for others' approval. Many continue to live and work as though they had not heard the knell but I no longer hesitate to call that a kind of living death. Something is being signalled but they either cannot or will not hear it. Others hear but, after a few gestures in a new direction, decide they were mistaken. It is no easy matter to accept that the responsibility for the quality of the afternoon of my life lies within me.

Mid-life is a time of tremendous potential, of opportunities and perils. Questions, which may begin to occur in one's early thirties, are raised about many of the activities and relationships of one's life. Marriage is no exception. Whether such questions, about how we are spending what is ever more clearly our only life, become constructive or destructive depends in great part upon the attitude we take towards them. Should they be acknowledged or concealed? Are they inevitable or signs of instability? How we respond to them may be life-renewing or shattering. To conceal or deny the questions leads not to life but to either of two forms of death: one is the world of more booze, pills, affairs, gambling; the other is progressive boredom, sloth and rigidity. The ultimate choice, as Erik Erikson has shown, is either despair or a growing sense of the integrity of one's life. Which of these it will be depends to a great extent on how we respond to the bell's toll. Many will be so intimidated by the life-shattering potential of a new direction that they will decline inherent possibilities for renewal. These possibilities need not, as we shall see, be absolute in order to be important.

How shall we approach the issues between mid-life husbands and wives, acknowledging that such issues are partly universal and partly arise from distinctive contemporary American attitudes about marriage? Let's go back to several things we said in the second chapter. There we suggested that, in a society where the rites of passage into adulthood are imprecise at best, youth are nudged out of the impasse of adolescence by the appeal of certain illusions about the future. Young people, understandably bewildered by the vast range of careers and partners from which to choose, are lured into commitments which promise that these activities and relationships will be fulfilling. In a society incapable of conferring adult status and roles to its youth these are the means which we have devised. Not all options are offered to young people, and little encouragement is given to deviant roles, but the promise of fulfillment in work and marriage is adequate to mobilize most middle-class youth.

In that discussion we noted an unfamiliar symptom: some of them are experiencing disillusionment prematurely. Before experiencing the partial rewards which inhere in both marriage and work they are abandoning the illusions. This will have serious consequences for sustaining a sense of purpose in one's 20's and 30's about earlier commitments. More important it will undermine the basis for much of the creative negotiation of mid-life issues. Young adults will have abandoned the illusions about career and relationships before they know their benefits; and it is appreciation of the gains, however partial, of such commitments which makes possible their serious re-evaluation.

Under ordinary circumstances it is part of the definition of · mid-life that this is a time, varying with individuals, when one becomes aware of the limitations of one's youthful, ideological commitments. Disliking ambiguity, tolerance for which I assume to be the distinguishing role of adulthood, youth's commitments all tend to be absolutistic. One will even consciously suppress negative evidence regarding both one's chosen career and partner in order to be, or at least to appear, wholehearted. I simply take youth to be that stage of life when one is unable to acknowledge either the multiple motivations people have for everything they do or the adequacy of imperfect motivation to sustain effort in most situations. The ability to acknowledge, and even to be grateful, for such imperfection is a fruit of experience, which is precisely what youth lacks.

It is this realization to which the mid-life person is beginning to come. And it is healthy. It signals the end of an era: the passing of youthful illusions about the capacity of any single activity or relationship, or any combination of these, to fulfill. In the light of experience the very expectation of fulfillment must give way to new ways of thinking about one's work and love.

To put it this way may sound like a call to abandon ship, and we see evidence that this reaction is widespread. I have no such intention. Rather, I believe that such realization of the fraudulence of youthful absolutistic illusions frees one to acknowledge the real gains and limitations experienced at the shop and at home. For as long as the absolute standard prevailed there was no hope: nothing or nobody measured up to one's dreams; there was no possibility of assigning importance to and being nourished by one's modest, ordinary accomplishments. Ultimately, such perfectionism results either in Erikson's despair, despising both the world and oneself, or it is abandoned in favor of a real world in which there are always both gains and losses, a world in which imperfection persists to the very end without inhibiting one's efforts to improve.

It is to this real world that mid-life aspires. As one is able to recognize that less than fulfilling experiences have yielded undeniable and precious gains such a world is increasingly reachable. For example, I don't know what others may have dreamed about the fulfillment in becoming a parent but I do know that I have derived benefits from being a father provided by no other experience of my life. To those today who abhor the notion of parenting I can only say that they could be depriving themselves of one of life's most instructive, real experiences.

Unique to being a parent is the realization that the child exists because its parents willed it. This involves not only special parental responsibilities but the gradual realization that, whatever your capabilities, you can't share with this child more than you have. To this experience of personal limits one must add awareness of one's capacities for both making mistakes and injuring the other. The latter are made bearable by the gradual realization that even one's worst mistakes are rarely fatal. Given at least ordinary affection for one's children they prove more resilient than one might have thought. Add to this the child's gift of often unqualified affection and the case for being a parent can be persuasively argued. The desire to be a better parent or spouse, which does not include the possibility of perfection in either, is enhanced by what have been the gains from imperfect experiences.

The point is that at mid-life, as at all other transitional times of life, one can only enter upon new insecurity on the basis of previous security. It is on the basis of a reasonably adequate self-identity that the adolescent is able to venture into the uncertainty of intimate relationships with others. To the extent that one must conceal one's imperfections and deny those of the other the conditions are present for the introduction of absolutistic expectations. But even these deceptions, which will be reviewed and probably abandoned at mid-life, are the source of gains out of which a sense of security is built. As one is able to acknowledge the gains one realizes that the conditions are present for the next risks one must take: to evaluate one's relationships to determine what deserves to endure and what needs to be changed. These matters are usually clearer with reference to one's children, who may have reached maturity and actively need to redefine their relationship to parents, than to one's partner. So, let's consider some of the ways in which the wife/husband relationship may need to be reviewed.

Three such areas seem to be universal: concealment in roles, habituated responses to the other, and the realization that change comes hard. I am assuming that agreement about the first two will be relatively easy and that extended discussion of the latter will best be deferred to later in the chapter.

Over the years it gradually became apparent to me that it was all too possible, at times almost inevitable, to hide from one's spouse behind necessary domestic roles. Since parenthood is, like marriage itself, a role for which we are prepared largely by having been a child in another family, I was unaware of all of the ways in which I would be called upon to grow as a father. What I hadn't realized was that my wife and I would bring into our marriage different perceptions of the way people behaved as parents. We had to learn to adjust our inherited perceptions of being husband and wife to the realities of our respective capabilities. There is much to be said for couples having time to work through some of these universal issues before having to learn to be parents. The lessons rarely came easily.

The unanticipated need to grow, for which we were little prepared, is a good excuse for hiding behind domestic functions. That today's parents can be exceptionally busy (see Irma Bombeck's, *The Grass Is Always Greener Over the Septic Tank*, for a poignant description of the demands of suburban life) makes it quite easy to avoid the partner. But the busyness is almost always an excuse for refusing to address those differences which are in all marriages. The busyness conceals the fact, at least until mid-life's unmasking, that many people see conflict as both undesirable and dangerous. Many seem to believe that the presence of conflict means the absence of love. While I would not deny the danger which is latent in all conflict—the evidence of battered wives and children is too serious to warrant treating conflict casually—it is unavoidable. It does not represent the absence of love unless love is not, at least in part, the means with which the conflict is resolved. The questions are these: Is a person prepared to deal reasonably readily with whatever demands his/her attention? Is a spouse able to recognize that marriage and the roles which it creates, are not the means for avoiding conflict? Is it instead a chosen relationship within which conflicts may be faced and, subject to the personal resources available, resolved? Unable to understand marriage in this way a couple will reach mid-life with few reassuring experiences of conflict-resolution. Having known some success they may reasonably hope to continue to grow together once many of the parental roles have passed. Lacking such security it hardly seems that a marriage would survive the challenges of mid-life's conflicts. Such couples may stay together but with less prospect, in that relationship, of their continuing maturation as persons.

One word needs to be said about the passing of parental roles. It often isn't quite that simple. Rarely are children as completely gone as I may have implied. Even assuming the absence in one's children of any dramatic problems in their adulthood, further maturation is required of their parents. The desperate efforts of grandparents to look and act as young as their children seem to me to illustrate the refusal of a generation of men and women to act its age. By so refusing the maturation which time's passage makes possible they withhold from their children and grand-children the distinctive gifts which nobody else may have to give.

The second of the aspects of marital life which may come under mid-life review is the tendency for couples to have developed habituated responses to each other: "I just knew you'd say that!"; or "Isn't that just like him/her!" Before condoning the implied condemnation of habit, however, let's acknowledge that familiarity with another's tendencies and a certain behavioral consistency are not inherently evil. As always, the difficulty arises at the point at which enough of anything becomes too much. The difficulty is always with the balance: the consistency which enables us to rely on each other becomes noxious when innovativeness has been sacrificed to predictability. By doing so, one has eliminated risk in favor of security and the effect is boring. But our mania for flexibility and creativity should not blind us to the utility and worth of a person who is strong enough within his or her character to be able to act consistently. Something similar should be said on the other side of this issue. Familiarity need not breed contempt. Many of the kindnesses of which people are capable, both in and out of marriage, are possible only if we know enough about the other to know what might please them. Neither chance nor expenditure assures that a gift will be well received as much as does some knowledge of the person for whom the gift is intended.

So, familiarity with and the general predictability of the other are resources which we all draw on every day. We could not function otherwise. Pushed to extremes, however, they repre-

sent serious issues which it is the business of mid-life to expose.
If we are always able to predict the other's response we may
either have a spouse who has become overly rigid or we may be
looking to see in the other, only what we want to see. It can also
happen that a highly erratic and unreliable person prompts the
partner to more stability than might otherwise have been the
case. "Somebody in this house has to look after the bank
account; we'd be broke all the time if I acted as s/he always
does!" By such subtle and not so subtle pressures are lives
reshaped and patterns established which have a way of
becoming domestic traps.

The function of mid-life is to acknowledge those points at
which patterns feel like traps, at which all capacity for surprise
seems to have disappeared from the marriage. It is not that most
people at mid-life are "up" for endless surprises. This would
probably be more tiring, if not as boring, as the wholly
predictable life. But, with the realization that there is but the
remainder of one's years in which to live, the mid-life yearning
for the possibility of some surprises is not inappropriate.

The real surprise for many mid-life couples is where the
potential for nourishing surprise is to be found. The sale of sex
manuals, with their assumption that any deficiency in marital
life lies in inadequate technique, suggests that many look to the
wrong resources. While most mid-life couples' sexual relations
probably could be enhanced by greater knowledge, the issue is
not ignorance. The task is to see the continuing sexual
relationship of a couple in the larger context of their relationship
to each other as people. It is not satisfactory sex which makes for
a rewarding relationship; it is a growing, and therefore
struggling, relationship which makes for enduringly satisfying
sexual life. Habituated responses to each other in the kitchen
probably parallel comparable responses in bed. In such a case
the latter only compounds the frustration of the former. The real
surprise, which should not really surprise us, is that the key to
the renewal of relationships is internal. Individuals are no more
renewed by techniques than it is possible to revivify a marriage
by merely external changes. The move to separate beds or
bedrooms deals neither with issues of sexuality nor solitude.
The source of our sense of well-being is internal and, just as

individual well-being is enhanced by self-acquaintance, relationships are enhanced only by mutual sharing. The potential for this is greater at mid-life than earlier and, if acted on, increases with the passage of time.

It is with the hope of recovering some of the spontaneity, some of the imagination, some of the evidences of caring, that once characterized a relationship that mid-life must review the patterns and traps of present marital life. If there have been patterns of mutuality, however limited, and if there is still some non-patterned creativity, then there have been gains. There is enough security with which to risk asking basic questions about the imaginable future character of the relationship. This seems to me healthy and probably something that couples over the centuries have done. In *Those Who Love*, Irving Stone offers somewhat fictionalized evidence of the efforts of John and Abigal Adams to work through such issues. At all transitional times the ability to risk is predicated on security previously gained. It is the security derived from earlier gains that makes self-sacrifice possible; otherwise, what might be thought to be risk-taking is a form of self-destruction.

The third area of possible mid-life review, of which there will be further discussion later, has to do with the possibility of change. It comes hard. The evidence of the difficulty may be piled as high as a Minnesota snowbank in January but it still fails to convince. Notions about our great flexibility, our limitless capacity for growth, are very deeply engrained. They often seem ineradicable and that is both a curse and a blessing.

It is a curse which has encompassed an ever larger segment of the population as increasing numbers of people have stayed longer in schools. For the assumption underlying modern higher education is that if you know a thing you can do it. Such an awareness of limits as the seventeenth century settlers brought with them quickly gave way to the assumption that anything is possible. And, for as long as there was land to the west to be expropriated, the physical expansion of America seemed to support the notion that there was nothing we could not do. Despite the efforts of a few to suggest that Alaska represents today what Frederick Jackson Turner saw in the frontier, the fact is that the frontier has not existed for a century. Even the myth to which it lent credence has been dying for almost that long. But, if the awareness of the reality of physical limits is progressively undeniable, we hang on doggedly to notions about our personal capability for growth. It is a curse because, given our large-mindedness about potential, it makes it difficult for modest changes to be nourishing. By shielding us from a radically tragic sense of life such expectations also cut us off from an appreciation for slight change. With us, regrettably, it is too often all or nothing at all.

Our assumption about our capacity for growth, especially if it can be made more modest, may also be a blessing. Fatalists we are not. And the very education which we are in the process of universalizing has the virtue of encouraging us to seek solutions. Clearly, they are not always available, as every President and Secretary of State eventually discovers, and we need to be equipped both to persist in the search and to realize that not all problems are solvable. Few problems in the realm of significant relationships have solutions. There may be solutions to external, expecially formal, difficulties; where people are involved it would be well to rid ourselves of such absolutistic notions. In marriages there is always the possibility of change, if there is the will, but that will must always encompass that fact that somebody, preferably two bodies, will have to pay for the change. Even for an enduring, minor change to occur there are no bargain basements. Since we are talking about the reorganization of the inner life of two persons there are no giveaways. Somebody must suffer for the sake of the limited gain. These realizations are constraints rather than imprisoning chains and we can live better with their limitations than with limitless illusions. The only question is whether or not we can learn to be satisfied at any given time with limited improvements. We need to become able to feel good about the fact that it is only gradual increments of growth of which we are capable. That no eventual limits to the potential for cumulative change may be specified is the source of hope. But is that enough to motivate anyone?

How do people respond to the challenge of growth? Rarely are they utterly clear-cut. Even the person whose refusal to grow seems total probably has some lingering desire to improve. Nobody is ever so far gone as to be oblivious to the claims of others or of his/her own humanity. The desire to be more lovable and loving is, I believe, ineradicable. Nor should we assume that the person who accepts the challenge does so unequivocally. That may indeed be the basic response, and that response is what matters, but there will be faltering and refusal as well. The demands of the process are such that, however desirable the results may look, everybody has at least second thoughts about persisting. But, such reversals no more assure defeat than does a flicker of effort on the part of one who initially refused the challenge signal victory. We all waffle.[2]

We do not, I believe, need to concern ourselves at length with those who basically refuse the challenge. The Sunday supplements cover all too thoroughly the self-destructiveness of alcohol and drugs, gambling, pills, successive affairs, and so forth. When both spouses decline the challenge we see either progressive distancing from each other or mutual mis-use. The tragedy is that the costs of such refusal to grow are not confined to the particular couple. While there is much more to Equus than the character and relationship of Adam's parents, the play illustrates the destructiveness to their son of their refusals to grow. The harsh father's substitution of pornographic movies for his relationship to an aloof wife impoverished more than their lives. The challenge to growth is endless and the price of refusal is paid both by the refusers and by all the lives to which they are related. Rarely is self-destructiveness confined to one person.

Some of the action taken by those who accept the challenge to growth may not initially appear to be all that constructive or forthright. Divorce, for example, may be the only constructive course open to some couples. Nor does resignation, about which we shall speak at length later, appear to be all that constructive. But resignation, implies a recognition of the reality of limits and by so doing may be the only attitude which enables one to be capable of change. So, both divorce and resignation are among the positive resources which may be drawn upon by those who affirm the challenge to growth. They represent the desire to move beyond impasse by abandoning unproductive patterns.

Perhaps the most important first step that can be taken by those who want to work at their relationship is to recognize the adverse effects of unrealistic expectations. Two of these may illustrate. The expectation that marriage should be free of confict thwarts the capacity of many couples to grow. Even people who grew up in turbulent families expect that their marriage will be different. Two possible explanations of such a phenomenon come to mind: our inability to acknowledge how determined our lives are by past experience and our mistaken view that love means the absence of conflict. This is poor equipment for people entering or trying to sustain that relationship which contains virtually every conceivable basis on which disagreement is possible. Consider the range of potentially divisive issues with which every couple must deal: how to spend time, money, and energy; how to relate to society, from the neighbors next door to the needs of the Third World; what values shall inform personal behavior and public attitudes. From agreeing on the time for which the morning alarm should be set to deciding when to go to bed there are issues to be negotiated. The potential for conflict is ubiquitous; the only issue is whether or not a couple will be able to find responses which are more frequently constructive than destructive. A sense of humor, that is, the ability to resist inflating every disagreement, cannot be overvalued.

The demand for perfect motivation is another unrealistic expectation with which mid-life couples have to come to terms. Perhaps the most helpful observation for those addressing such expectations was made by Dr. Howard Rome, psychiatrist at the Mayo Clinic: "All human behavior is overmotivated." That we always have more reasons for doing something than we actually need to accomplish the action is the corrective for all perfectionism. To expect singleness of motive is unrealistic. We should be moving in the direction of greater consistency but to assume that this requires or will ever result in utter purity of heart is misguided. What mid-life couples may need to acquire is the ability to be grateful for what might once have been disapprovingly called halfheartedness. We must be able to recognize the variety of motivations one brings to every occasion and to strive to be in touch with those which are most relevant. This does not mean there is no place for rules or duties or laws. It would be impossible to function without them but they are not the key to our well-being. That key is in the willingness to be imperfect without being resigned to present imperfection.

There are innumerable other unrealistic expectations which have adverse effects. We spoke of illusions about self-fulfillment through marriage and/or parenthood, and of the error of equating sexual satisfaction with skill in techniques. The expectation that a rigorously disciplined family will lead to domestic harmony might be another to add to the list. The point, however, is not to be exhaustive—this is no manual for troubled couples—but to suggest some of the expectations which may need to be reviewed by the mid-life couple who have accepted the challenge of growth. The recognition that an aspect of a relationship has been troubled, while a necessary first step, does not assure that the resources are present to deal with it. Too much time may have elapsed; too many injuries may have for too long gone uncomforted; one party may have too long a memory, the other too short. But nobody should generalize about when a relationship has reached the point of no return. The tolerances vary with individuals: somebody's "too much" is somebody else's "just enough." We do well if we are able to identify some of the issues, leaving particular couples to discover their import for themselves.

The key to the successful outcome of any mid-life evaluation of marriage lies in the couple's capacity for assenting to the limited possibilities for continuing maturation of the relationship. That there are limits many married people have long recognized and can be quite explicit about identifying in others. I, however, am urging the need for two additional things: admitting my limits and discovering the satisfaction of modest gains. In addition to this admission, we must realize that our capacities for growth are either enlarging because we have taken some advantage of them or they are becoming more constricted because we failed to do so. That is, the range of our freedom is either becoming greater through the exercise of it or is becoming less by neglect. The need is neither to deny limits nor to find satisfaction only in the quantity of one's enlargement of limits. Rather, it is to discover satisfaction in some movement. Most relationships are improvable less by abrupt, dramatic changes, which are impossible to sustain, than by modest, repeated changes which have the potential for enduring. A slight change in the compass-heading will, on a long journey, result in arrival at a quite different destination. Radical change in that heading unsettles all aboard.

In the not so remote past men and women may have tolerated much less growth in marriage than is expected today. What was then tolerable might now be quite unacceptable. Not only were the very terms on which they posted their banns quite different from ours—the subservience of the wife to the husband being but the most obvious—but the problems with which they had to cope are not ours. Think of the sheer task of survival in an adverse environment. Who can make light of the inhospitable land in Sweden, as depicted in *The Emigrants*, which men and women attempted to farm? While the soil along the St. Croix River in that film's sequel was deep and rich, the tasks were such that initial survival demanded all of their energy. There was an enviable heroism then but early deaths temper any inclination to romanticize.

Having seen these Swedish films I experienced a special irony as I read the following while flying to Minneapolis directly over their valley.

> Mounting absenteeism and declining enthusiasm for work among their employees are prompting many Western industrialists to begin serious studies on problems caused by these reevaluations of jobs and life itself.
>
> Western developments of this kind are getting increasingly hard for the Japanese industrialists to ignore. The Japanese spirit of diligence at work . . . has recently shown some signs of changing. . . .
>
> The rising level of education is generating a strong sense of doubt among an increasing number of younger, educated employees as to the meaning of the jobs to which they are assigned.[3]

As our descent brought us within sight of where the survival struggles of this particular group of immigrants took place, the magazine editorialized.

> In many cases, people are seeking out employment . . . which offers a boost to the human dignity standard, as well as to the product output. Good hours, good benefits, a little money to burn

and a holiday bonus notwithstanding, the good ships Business and Industry are throttling up for what may be their biggest test yet.[4]

Within less than a century we have moved from invariant survival needs on the frontier to the varied expectations of the upwardly mobile. It is obvious that what we look for in both work and family is radically different from those settlers only a few generations removed from us. That what we may desire, especially from our marriages, demands sacrifice analagous to theirs we recognize less easily. In our relationships the cost of the very improvements we desire both fascinates and repulses us. Those who survived the frontier probably experienced some similar ambivalence but the survivors refused to be determined by their fears. It was not just the homesick bride who died because of her inability to be more fascinated than repulsed by the tasks of the new land. The costs of survival and the costs of improvement have always required people to be led by the possibilities to which they were attracted rather than immobilized by risks they dreaded.

Change and growth are always simultaneously fascinating and terrifying for at least two reasons: they involve both gains and losses and we realize that the choice is always to grow or to die. There is no stasis, no enduring stability. That which winter freezes solid gives way to the instability of spring. We are either involved in ever more of reality or we are affirming less of it. There was no standing for the St. Croix immigrants—they either farmed more or the forest recovered what it had lost—and the same is true for us. We are either in touch with more of ourselves and have that much more to share or we know and can give less. It is not possible to know in advance either the precise nature of the gains from growth, the satisfactions which will result, the exact character of the losses, or their consequent distress. We can try to minimize the latter but the only thing we can be sure of is that we are responding to a need for growth. Whether or not that certainty will suffice will be determined by the depth of our commitment to grow.

The trouble is that we have few cultural aids to assist our tentative inclinations to affirm the demands of maturation. Who has seen a popular TV sitcom whose outcome could not be imagined early in the first segment? If this and professional athletics are the primary sources from which the public derives its insights into the human situation I shall have to opt for the sports. The outcome of the games is not predetermined. Chance and serendipity are still factors. I can think at the moment of only two television programs in which the imperfection of the participants was both evident and intrinsic to the production. The first was a film of rehearsals prior to the relaunching of the career of Peggy Lee. Even though it was undoubtedly edited, here one had access to the unfinished product. Here one could see the conflicts between those who were planning the event; one was even allowed to see and hear mistakes. It was significant entertainment and instruction. Television programs to the contrary notwithstanding, life is not smooth-edged and slick and this rare program celebrated that fact. Leonard Bernstein's programs for children intended to let the viewer in on rehearsals but he is so much more polished that much was obscured that might have been useful to the young and the not so young who need to know that imperfection is not disaster.

The other program that may have helped viewers to affirm the unavoidable need for change was the six-part series, Six American Families, which had the regional, economic, racial, and religious diversity that is representative of the American scene. The often insoluble difficulties and the limited personal resources with which the families tried to deal with their situations were credibly shown. While little in this series was as entertaining as most of the Peggy Lee program, all of the presentations were potentially instructive to couples at almost any stage of the life cycle.

It is my most important assumption that, inasmuch as we can know it, the main purpose of life is to enable us to be in ever deeper, more appropriate, and rewarding relationship with ourselves, with others, and with the world. While there have been endless efforts within both philosophy and religion to find ways to overcome the fact of separation, my experience is largely informed by the distinctively Jewish/Christian emphases on the normativeness of relationships. Because of this understanding we cannot deny the importance either of the self or of the other.

History is strewn with schemes which resolved this tension either in favor of the individual or the group but such alternatives were doomed because each attempts to obscure half of reality. Collectivist panaceas leave insufficient room for the individual, as contemporary totalitarianisms demonstrate, and individualistic panaceas ignore the extent to which all lives are rooted in society. It would be so convenient to let go of one side of the tension, to be able to lose oneself either in angelic transcendence or by submersion into the herd, but it is not possible to get rid of the burden and glory of one's humanity in these ways. While there probably will always be programs urging one or the other we should not be seduced by them because we cannot become either angels or animals. To be a person is to live amphibiously: on the one hand deeply grounded in the natural world, mortal, and subject to great passions; and on the other capable of considerable self-transcendence and self-sacrifice. It is no wonder that such a creature has fashioned both totem animals and the myth of Aquarius.

If life in relationship is the burden and glory of our humanity we need next to remind ourselves of some of the essential characteristics of a human relationship. Primarily it assumes that the people entering the relationship are equals. While item-for-item equality is not true even for identical twins, we should not confuse equality with identity. Any yearning for identity is a temptation to escape one's humanity. As the primary characteristic of a human relationship the assumption of equality means that there is no inherent basis for treating the other as an object. In day to day life there are many occasions in which we objectify each other—for instance, it is I who shovel the snow today while she makes breakfast—but there is never reason in relationship for dealing with each other as objects.

From this we see another characteristic of a human relationship: it is entered into freely. Not only is there no grounds for lording it over the other but there is no excuse for coercion, however subtle, to bring about the relationship. It is from one's inner freedom that one chooses or declines to engage another person. From this it follows that, within a freely entered relationship, one seeks to be as open to the other as possible. The point of having freely chosen and been chosen is to be as fully present to each other as possible. Assuming the trustworthiness of the relationship there is increasing desire not to hide things otherwise concealed. Both for oneself and for the other one desires to be as fully present as possible. The object of such a freely entered, mutually equal, progressively open relationship is to enhance the freedom of both parties. Human friendship presupposes the exercise of freedom for the sake of its enlargement. As in most life situations it is freedom which is endangered in marriage, freedom by which we are both terrified and endlessly fascinated, freedom which searches for contexts within which to create something new.

Based on this understanding we may consider the potential in marriage for the enhancement of human freedom. In the light of many people's marital experience this may seem an absurd statement. Can we, however, be guided by the experience of those who may have neither such vision of the relationship nor appreciation for its demands? It may also be objected that my understanding of marriage's primary purpose ignores many of the functions ordinarily associated with marriage, such as reproduction, the maintenance of social stability, and the orderly transfer of property. There are indeed many possible consequences of a sound vision of the marital relationship but these are secondary considerations. Since it is impossible to define the limits of any institution with absolute clarity some of the responsibilities added are appropriate and bearable, others are extrinsic and should be refused. (In light of the importance which I earlier gave to being a parent, I should acknowledge that I do not consider reproduction an inherent responsibility of marriage. I believe that couples should include the possibility of having children as part of their freely chosen relationship but there could well be reasons peculiar to circumstances which could justify a contrary decision.) I have come to understand that the intrinsic purpose of the marital relationship is involved in the making of *human* lives. Many years ago a book was published in England entitled, *Real Life Is Meeting*. Those four words state that conviction which informs my high valuation of marriage: in that relationship we have potentially the best condition for lives to meet and mature.

Since we are discussing marital relationships at mid-life we now are able to see the basic question which has to be faced and resolved: what happens to the mutuality which first brought a couple together? I have to assume that, whatever the extraneous factors may have been, they married with some expectations of mutuality. In addition to prudence, lust, fear, tradition, desperation, and so forth, I believe that there was at least a minimal sense that in the relationship there was the possibility for personal growth as well as the enjoyment of living with another. The couple had reason to hope for the fulfillment of their respective lives and for benefitting others through their relationship. Ultimately, this is a yearning which informs all human life and, despite the most adverse experience, is inextinguishable. Evidence from the Holocaust indicates the irrepressibility of this hope. In an early book, originally published as *From Death Camp to Existentialism*, Viktor Frankl says that the individual's capacity to survive concentration camps was largely a factor of his or her ability to sustain that hope. When, for whatever reason, that hope was extinguished an otherwise healthy person could die in a few hours. Whether or not some such hope for mutuality endures is the question to be faced by the married in mid-life. How real was the original bond? Has there been evidence over the years that the trustworthiness, which originally warranted the risk of marriage, is really there? And, if present, is it there in sufficient quantity to justify continuing a relationship in the predictably different years ahead?

These are difficult questions for couples to face. They are not, however, the most difficult. The harder question is this: Am I ready to abandon my efforts to re-shape the other to my liking? While it is theoretically a question which could be asked much earlier in life that is unlikely. It requires the passage of time and the accumulation of a great deal of evidence to be able to recognize what one has been attempting to do. Yet additional time and more of the same experience may be necessary before one is able to admit both the impossibility and the utter inappropriateness of efforts to remake the other in our own image. Such an admission is a prelude either to the abandonment of the partner, which can be accomplished as well by neglect as by departure, or to recognizing what one has been doing. Facing up, which may be one of the supremely human acts, is extremely difficult.

The timing for admitting the hopelessness of such efforts will vary with individuals. Some never stop; others never really recognize what they're trying to do. Here again, it is instructive to turn back to those adolescent years in which so many of the patterns of adult life began to take shape.

In discussing adolescence we have said that the primary task is to fashion an identity with which one can be comfortable and which the significant people in our life find credible. That such identities contain elements of deception—of ourselves as well as others—is assumed. Such deceptions need not be all that important providing we understand that further experience should enable us to correct our self-understanding. The problem to be seen, in aggravated form in some people and in all to a lesser extent, is our resistance to learning about ourselves from experience. A source of this resistance is the failure to understand that it is in the nature of identity-formation to be imperfect. Lacking this understanding many people learn too well to conceal those aspects of themselves which did not conform to their apparent identity. This entrapment is compounded by the fact that, in the interest of success, we are strongly encouraged to pretend certainty. Ostensibly this singlemindedness constitutes strength. Thus, a quarrel which may seem to be purely domestic often should be a quarrel with societal emphases on concealment.

Ideally, young people realize two things: that there is much more to them than "shows" and that what can be seen is adequate to elicit confirmation from the significant people in their lives. It is this combination which makes one capable of entering into those intimate relations which hold the potential for hope-filled commitments. While Erikson's discussion of intimacy makes quite clear that full sexual relations are not part of his definition, they are always a possibility. Unfortunately, both in and out of marriage much sexual intercourse lacks the viable identity which is intimacy's pre-condition.

The point we must stress is that the capacity for intimacy, for meaningful if incomplete commitment to another, includes the acknowledgment of imperfection. This is a major step in one's maturation for it means that one has found the means, *in relationship,* to move beyond an ideological insistence on perfection. To be capable of intimacy means that, recognizing both one's own and the other's imperfection, one can meaningfully give and receive. Can the importance of relationships to human life be more clearly stated than this: they are the means by which presently imperfect people may share their imperfection with the reasonable expectation of endless improvement of self-understanding and increasing openness to the other? Is this not the source of one's availability to all others? Is it not the source of that most precious of human gifts, the ability to care? If so, we may identify intimacy as the means by which our kinship with all imperfect others is nourished.

Now we may see why all efforts to make over the other in our image are inappropriate. (Incidentally, I assume that the use of language related to sexual intercourse often reveals basic life attitudes. To what extent is talk of "making" someone a predictor of future efforts to make over? I do not want to suggest that I believe that the full range of sexual experience can be confined within genteel language. But some language is inadequate precisely because its instrumental character does violence both to the complexity and the mutuality of the act.) What enabled the initial intimacy was not the assumption about either the perfection of the partners or of their need to be alike. Enough similarity of outlook and expectation (without attempting to define what is enough), is clearly a precondition for an enduring commitment. But is not the very fact of difference one of the most important lures to intimacy? It is the opportunity to be in touch with another, and different, human being which is the appeal of all relationships. It is the prospect of receiving and being received by a comparably whole, comparably flawed person that empowers us to acts of friendship. The inability to so enter relationships only results in progressive distancing from others. The developmental tragedy of this is the resultant distancing from oneself. The conditions for deepening self-acquaintance having been lost, the person has no alternative to progressive concealment, feigned strength and eventual despair. The basis for a caring concern for the future has been lost in the deceptions of past and present. The failure to achieve a generative attitude towards the future results in progressive stagnation.

To avoid this we must emphasize that there are learning problems at the time of marriage. Since there is the tendency to be self-justifying, and since we know only how our parents behaved, we tend to relate to our spouse with those childhood-formed expectations in mind. Since both parties bring somewhat different experiences and expectations into the relationship there is obviously much to learn and to unlearn. A viable marriage might be defined as one in which enough of the requisite learning and unlearning occurs soon enough. Unfortunately, we are not easily resigned to the uniqueness to which we were initially attracted in the other. These dynamics, which are among the important issues which come up for mid-life review, contain the potential for dramatic transformation of individual lives and of any relationship.

The word which I used to describe my own awakening to this situation was resignation. By it I meant to describe my realization of how wrongheaded I had been in my efforts to make over my wife in my own image. That realization included a two-fold admission: that I was too imperfect to be a model for anybody else and that it was often the beauty of her character which I had been trying to modify. By resignation I was trying to acknowledge both my unsuccessful efforts and their utter inappropriateness. Having used the word in a public talk about these matters I learned that resignation has negative connotations for most people. Unable to appreciate the positive qualities I intended—the pleasure of being able to discontinue a hopeless effort and the great joy of realizing what a mistaken project it had been—others preferred the word acceptance.

Whether or not there is one suitable word to describe the experience is vastly less important than the realization of what one has been attempting. It is the uniqueness of the other which we both should and do value in any relationship. It is the precious inwardness of a human life that we are talking about and such changes as may occur are controlled from within. The analogy of good therapy may be useful at this point. In my experience very little that the counsellor says, except to clarify by restating what has already been revealed, contributes to the healing. Good counselling is not a process of telling the other what is wrong and what s/he needs to do. People in need often leave after such an experience, with profuse expressions of thanks, and never return. They will not tolerate being reshaped from without because it involves the abandonment of the final sanctuary of self-respect. Only those discoveries matter to which the counsellee is able to come. Though assisted by a wise listener, the agenda for change and the ways of looking at it are determined by the person in search of greater wholeness.

This was the point at which, as the British say, the penny dropped. This was the point at which I began to be aware of the great gift which mid-life was trying to give. It is the gift of love. Finally, after years of the fatiguing pretense of love I got a glimmer of what love means: it is the recognition that the other is not modifiable. Love is the glad acceptance of the other's unassailable uniqueness. That it is not just unique but unassailably so is crucial to an understanding of love's toughness. It cannot be coerced. It can only be freely given or withheld. For example, one of the reasons I was originally attracted to, and have often since been grateful for, my wife is that she is a generous, considerate person. Over the years I made innumerable efforts to make her be more aggressive. When the penny dropped I saw two things clearly: that there is a rare beauty in this unique imperfection and that the changes I sought were largely to have served my very imperfect purposes.

The excitement and the terror of this discovery has yet one more feature. At mid-life we are confronted, both in work and in love, with the same question: What is it that I want to do? What is the growth which I hope to achieve? Less able than formerly to blame others or external factors for the quality of our lives, the person at mid-life may realize that the externalized life has been an abdication of personal responsibility. This is both heady and frightening. It is exciting to be aware, however briefly, that one is freer than one has long felt. However, fear enters as soon as one realizes that s/he neither knows what to do with the freedom nor whether the price is worth it. So few people have, over the years between adolescence and mid-life, kept in touch with their deep desires. Many have sought only those things which the system has taught us to want. Others are ill-prepared to begin at mid-life to identify their own wants because they have been led to believe that it is wrong to pursue one's own desires. They have been guided in their behavior by the needs and desires of others, such as their children or their social responsibilities. From a very early stage of life one must learn to balance one's own desires with those of others.

The realization of the inappropriateness and impossibility of wanting to reshape the other may lead to the crucial realization that the only reshaping of which one is capable is of oneself. The ultimate challenge at mid-life is that, if things are to be different, it is I who must grow. Nobody can do this for me nor can I blame the failure of it to happen on anybody else. It is my job, and mine only, to struggle with those qualities in me which hurt the other and impoverish the relationship. Central to this job is neither exhortation nor social pressure but the undeniable sense that, even as I am, I am somewhat accepted by the other. This is love's paradoxical gift: to free us for change by affirming us as we are.

This is why I believe that discussions of mid-life are both so popular and so incomplete: they are popular because it seems as though anything were possible, as though one had been given *carte blanche;* incomplete because the ball really is back in one's own court and one is faced, perhaps for the last time, with the question of what, if anything, one wants to do about it. To recognize that one's spouse is not reducible to some aspect of oneself may create for him/her the conditions out of which change is possible. It will never be easy and we can't help but ask what sort of growth am I capable of which will enhance the partnership? This question, like most important issues in a marriage, will have to be worked at both together and separately. In some instances the issues will be comparatively simple, for instance the need to build into a common life regular opportunities for being together. These need not be extensive but they should be unmistakable occasions of being with and for each other. In my own marriage this began as a brief, daily time together before dinner. That it has grown into a mutually rewarding pattern of regular reading aloud we could not have foreseen. In other cases the required change may be comparatively difficult: the increasing tendency to depend on generous amounts of alcohol or other substitutes to enable people to unwind.

The point here is not to identify every issue with which couples may have to grapple in the course of their encounter with mid-life. My more general concern is that married people rediscover something of what it was that first gave hope to their relationship and discover where it was that the relationship began to be less rewarding. The decision to marry may be one of life's great risks. Whether or not people are able to sustain the commitment is determined by their capacity for review and continued risk-taking.

We say that what everybody ultimately wants is to be accepted just as and for what they are. I believe this. But it leaves the most important ingredient unclear: who am I? Only as I am increasingly clear about who I am, which gradually acquaints me with not just my attractive side but with what may be my unattractiveness, can I say meaningfully that I want to be accepted just as I am. The task is, in the light of ever more complete self-knowledge, to be self-accepting, and I contend that marriage, or some comparable relationship, is the means by which both self-acquaintance and self-acceptance become possible. We are unable, in isolation, to see ourselves clearly. Self-praise and self-condemnation are usually both inaccurate. We come to see ourselves most clearly in those committed relationships in which we are free to be our best and our worst, where there is the mutual trust to work at these matters. The family is the milieu in which both self-knowledge and, by finding that spouse and children do not abandon us because they know us, self-acceptance are nurtured.

We will never be fully accepted by our families, nor need we be. Enough acceptance from spouse and children is crucial but we must not burden one set of relationships with total responsibility for our sense of well-being. There is much more to any person than can be contained within even the best of families. The point is that I believe that there are some mutual acceptances which first gives couples reason to hope that the opportunity for endless self-acquaintance lies in their particular relationship. It is impossible and unnecessary to identify all of the ways in which we desire and need to know ourselves better. But, since self-ignorance means both the impoverishment of one's own life and one's relationships, let me suggest a few of the areas in which the marital relationship often provides the means for the partners to become better informed about themselves. (Note that the illustrations largely have to do with latent aspects of ourselves to which our society gives limited encouragement.) A growing marital relationship will at least do the following things: permit men and women, especially the former, to be more vulnerable; encourage men and women to be in touch with children and aged people; acknowledge both the grief which we feel for the world's suffering and the exhilaration for life which we experience doing such things as gardening, or skin-diving, or holding an infant; put men in touch with their feminine side and women in touch with their masculine side; find a place for both the rationality and the absurdity which is to be found in all lives; allow acknowledgement of rage, while finding substitutes for acting it out, and for the expression of the deepest tenderness without insisting on confining its expression to the family; help recognition of the presence within us of both ambition and sloth, of both caring and indifference. This list could be vastly enlarged and others would appropriately substitute for my illustrations. The point is that we see the endless growth which I believe everybody desires, and which it is marriage's central purpose to serve. Love is not just an end in itself. It is also the means by which crucial growth occurs. It is utterly non-sentimental though it cries when tears are appropriate and belly-laughs at other times. I am not sure whether or not such an understanding can be recovered in a society which has utterly sentimentalized love, but to my mind it is the end we should seek. It is the relationship that so desires the truth about both parties that it is willing to risk itself in the process. If the risk succeeds the relationship is enhanced; if it fails the relationship is shaken but not necessarily destroyed.

What in fact does destroy a marriage is the elimination of the willingness to take these truth-gaining risks. If I am correct about the hope which brings couples to marriage then the mid-life task for couples is to discover when and why they stopped risking. I suspect that the important external reasons are commonplace and fairly easily identified. Some, for example, have to do with becoming parents. There is much about having children which strengthens our inclination to prudence. There is so much that children don't yet know about the world. And if we desire an education for them, either for itself or for their advancement, parents usually feel that they must anticipate the cost of such schooling. Also, many of us do more than is probably necessary to conceal from our children our deficiencies and our flaws. These efforts are unavailing but we maintain the pretense. From the weight of this unsuccessful deception, as from lingering illusions about parenthood carried from our own childhood, we need to be relieved.

But becoming parents is not, I think, the chief external restraint of the capacity for taking risks. To work belongs that questionable honor. The principal breadwinner(s) finds it difficult not to give more time and energy to work than it deserves. So preoccupied can career-oriented people become (always, of course, with the "good" of the family as part of the motivation) that the time and energy required for pondering truth-related risking just doesn't exist.

It should clearly be stated that neither the making of a family nor the demands of career in themselves undermine the need for growth. Relationships with one's children and with the people and tasks at one's place of work do provide both the affection which encourages and the challenges which prompt growth. The problems for modern parents seem to be two-fold: the tendency to excessive commitments to family or work and the failure of couples to find ways to integrate into their relationship the problems, disappointments, satisfactions, and hopes of their lives. Thus, mid-life is, at the very least, a time when a great deal of catching up is long overdue. It is not unlike, but infinitely more complex than, trying to balance a long neglected, joint checking account.

The neglect of self and, concomitantly, the neglect of relationships is the ultimate and imperious issue underlying the trauma of mid-life. We are talking about men and women who, whatever their traditions of privacy, have long felt unable to be alone; men and women who, whatever their temperaments, have for too long let other demands supplant their desire to nurture that marriage which originally lured them from isolation to a hope-filled relationship.

A good marriage may not be the end of life but it can be a most important means by which men and women assist each other in their search for the properly inclusive goals of their lives. When marriage fails to further that search, whether by pretending to be life's goal or by refusing to risk itself for the sake of the search, it must be reviewed. When the resources cannot be found in the relationship to re-activate the search either the partners must be resigned to their fate or they must search elsewhere. Where some resources are at hand they will be adequate for the modest, gradual but crucial transformation of the marital relationship. It is my conviction that all activities, especially relationships, are rewarding to the extent that they are based upon some truth and moving in the direction of greater truthfulness. I am not naive about the difficulty of speaking and doing the truth, and am sure that there are exceptional occasions when intentional dishonesty may be appropriate. However, what we seek is more accurate self-perception and more accurate perceptions of others, for it is from this that more appropriate behavior is possible. It would be ultimately and rightly frustrating if a marriage was found to be predicated on some other assumption than the enlargement of truthfulness. A modest realization to the contrary is all that any couple needs.

As I have said earlier, I believe that a slight change of direction is both all that is possible and all that's required. It is the refreshment of a slight breeze, rather than refrigeration, that's needed on a hot summer night; the pleasure of warming one's hands before the fireplace rather than the furnace upon coming in from the cold. Given the ability to change direction slightly, to demonstrate some desire for modest risk-taking, may be enough to renew hope in a mid-life marriage. To act on such hope does not assure a trouble-free journey; just that the partners, themselves transformed by their common life, will arrive at a destination both like and unlike their port of departure.

CHAPTER 6

Relationships at Mid-life: Extra-marital

It was on a sunny, cold February afternoon that I realized the significance to me of three deaths which had occurred about a decade prior. I had, of course, known that I had lost people important to my life. Two of these were physical deaths—of my mother and a close friend of twenty-five years; the other was the death by his relocation to another part of the country of my closest adult friend. It was their recollection which helped me to recognize another of the central dimensions of the mid-life crisis: the realization that the important relationships of one's life are fragile. This awareness often leads to a central work of mid-life: sustaining friendships and a renewed interest in family, both the living and the dead.

On that winter day I was attending a conference with a group of students at a campsite on the St. Croix River. It was too cold to spend much time outdoors and, while partially confined with all those young people, I gradually became aware that I was the only adult along for the overnight. Over the past thirty years I had been along on many similar occasions with students, often as the sole adult. At such times I may have wished for adult companionship but I do not recall any sense of aloneness comparable to what I felt that afternoon. It was a familiar situation which led to an exceptional insight.

Yet there was something slightly different about that day. In pursuit of the topic set for discussion we had been asked to draw our lifeline so as to show those people who had been important to us. My first forty years were marked by progress which was disturbed by minor reversals reflecting, among other events, the deaths during my young manhood of several people who had been important in my life: my father, a cousin to whom I was close, and a high school chum. I had grieved these deaths but I had not been profoundly changed by them. At my father's death I was primarily uncertain as to how my mother would cope with being a widow. The deaths of two young friends saddened me primarily because I knew the emptiness of the homes from which they had been removed. Both families survived these deaths and I returned with alacrity to my demanding work and warm young family. My marriage and the eventual births of our children appeared on my graph as the most important relational changes in my life up to that time.

But, reflecting on the three deaths which occurred when I was in my early forties, I recorded a very sharp and long decline on my lifeline. The external circumstances were almost identical: in both instances I had lost a parent and two male friends. Why did the second set of losses have so much more dramatic an effect upon my emotional life? Actually, while I had thought myself realistically resigned to these deaths within a few months of each other, I began to experience something quite unique to me: a depression which I eventually came to recognize as one of mid-life's symptoms. To complete the picture I should add the fact that the first of our children went off to college at about that time and the second was to do so shortly. All these events combined to be more instructive than anything I had previously been required to learn.

Was the aloneness that I felt that wintry afternoon the result of recalling those deaths and realizing that I hadn't been able to ignore them as I had pretended? Or, did it arise from my inability to convey to students the profound importance of some relationships at some stages of our lives and the great grief that such losses can cause? For their part, the students were somewhat interested in what I had to share; certainly they were polite. But my tears bewildered them, and they reacted about as I had at their age to the death of my father and two young friends. Because the events I tried to recount were utterly unknown to them their reactions were minimal. They were more sympathetic with my distress but they made no pretense of comprehending it. They were young; I was at mid-life. They would console; they lacked the understanding to comfort. (When we are young we tend to assume not only that we will live forever but that all losses can be more than compensated for. As we get older we become more aware of our finitude and that there is no compensation for some losses. At twenty there is yet time to make many friends. At fifty there is simply less time left for cultivating relationships which we know do not mature quickly. I began to see the wisdom of the scouting song learned many years earlier during a similar outing; "Make new friends, but keep the old; One is silver, the other gold." It is not as easy as that but it points in the right direction.)

I have reported this experience for several reasons. It seems important to note the time delay which may accompany mid-life awareness. In this instance ten years passed before I was able to grasp the meaning of the loss of people who had been important in my life. Secondly, the insight came as a surprise. I might have chosen a better time and place had it been a matter of choice. Thirdly, that mid-winter camping experience made clear to me that, in addition to a review of one's work and marriage, mid-life is a time for paying closer attention to a variety of relationships. Long satisfied to have concentrated on the functional connections of one's life in the years after college, one may suddenly experience the need to add to the various roles in which one has been cast. Dissatisfaction with a largely function-defined existence—he's a lawyer, or she's a housewife—arises from the fact that it ignores, or causes one to minimize, many important aspects of one's being. There is so much more to any person than is acknowledged by, or relevant to, one's functions. One of the problems with most modern forms of work is that, by the importance attached to role-specializations, they contribute to a split between one's work and other activities. This may be necessary for efficiency in work which is both increasingly specialized and automated, but problems arise for those who try to make work increasingly the source of their life's meaning. Too great a burden is thereby imposed on too small an activity. If we are fortunate, though it needn't seem that at the time, experiences at mid-life will prompt us to pay attention to some areas of life long neglected. Friends and family will be among the chief of these.

So, in this chapter we shall look closely at two sets of important relationships outside of one's immediate household. That friendships and family connectedness do overlap with the relationships within a marriage was the reason that I spoke earlier of marriage as distinctive in degree only. A comparable capacity for intimacy characterizes both friendship and marriage. Actually, a good marriage may be the model for all friendship, but there are insights and strengths in friendships which both complement and could enhance most marriages. I shall confine myself largely to single-sex friendship, since this is primarily what I have known, but all that I shall have to say about such relationships are, in principle, applicable to heterosexual friendships. A good marriage is not, I believe, inherently threatened by such friendships.

Further, the search for family roots reveals that there are more relationships in a life than can be matched, or compensated for, in a marriage. Let me illustrate this point. As a person without living parents or siblings I had an important experience two years ago at my wife's family's grave plot. Having been affectionately related to her family for over thirty years, and lacking any comparable burial place of my own family, I felt both a kinship with these forebears who dated back to the mid-eighteenth century and a sense of connectedness with my own nameless forebears buried somewhere in Scotland. That the one set of ancestors had names and dates which the others lacked did not deprive me of an important sense of relationship to the past. It was equally important that this sense of connection with the past yielded a comparably vivid sense of my responsibility for the future. As my life had been cared for and informed by those who had preceded me, so was it my privilege to contribute to the well-being of those who would follow. I found myself willingly looking both ways. More of me than is often the case was taken into account on that warm summer afternoon in a dappled graveyard in upstate New York. I believe that I began then to understand for the first time those lines of Eliot.

> We shall not cease from exploration
> And the end of all our exploring
> Will be to arrive where we started
> And know the place for the first time.[1]

To this I would add: not just to know the place but to know the self who is the product of that and many other places. What besides the relationships of friends and family is capable of yielding such treasure?

While the importance of human friendship can hardly be overstated it was my experience over the twenty or so past years that the claims and joys of work and marriage preempted most of my time and energies. I have comparatively few regrets about the way I spent those decades. On balance, I enjoyed my experiences and did not utterly neglect friends from earlier times and other associations. As time permitted, I maintained correspondence with now physically remote friends of my youth. And, as travel permitted, I tried to see these and newer professional acquaintances. In large part, however, my ordinary life in a small college town contained most of what I needed and had time for: work was stimulating, family life was nourishing, activities were good. To the best of my knowledge I had been satisfied.

In combination with the deaths of my mother and a close friend of most of my adult life, it was the departure of my closest friend which informed me about the day-to-day importance of friends. With Tom's departure I lost not only a person with whom I enjoyed a variety of activities such as hiking, skiing, swimming, tennis but I also lost a man with whom distinctive conversation was possible. It was with him, and often with our wives as well, that aspects of my own life—past experiences, aspirations, matters about which I was troubled—could be uniquely shared. Since our work overlapped, some of our conversation was shop. It was with Tom that I first broached what we eventually saw to be mid-life's onset. It was a relationship in which both our strengths and weaknesses could be shared. It is relatively easy to find outlets for expressing one's strengths, though often not without arousing resentments. To have a friend who both celebrates one's achievements and is able to listen to one's shortcomings and complaints without being judgmental has been a much rarer experience. It is a death to lose such a friend and all too common a thing in a highly mobile society.

Perhaps the most important and distinctive characteristic of a friendship is the ability of both parties to listen. Inability to do so undermines many marriages and identifies any other relationship, no matter the time spent together, as only an acquaintance. Unless one is deaf we assume that we naturally can listen. That error of judgment does more than any single thing to keep relationships superficial. While I believe in the importance of learning to express ideas and feelings which are central to one's life, the precondition of such self-disclosure is the presence of a friend who can listen. Encounter groups may have their value but they should not be confused with friendship. Whatever one may divulge or hear over the course of an intensive weekend, and I would not belittle those who become more expressive in such settings, it is not the experience of friendship precisely because of its transiency. A friend is one who, given significant common history, can not only receive new information without judgment but is able to incorporate it into an enhanced relationship. The self-disclosures have not simply gone out into the air, which rewards us little; they have been listened to, accepted and made part of the friendship. It should not be assumed that friendship means or requires complete agreement on all controversial matters. One of my closest friends, whom I would trust in almost any situation, is a man with whom I disagree on many basic issues. The key to this, as to any friendship, is the mutual recognition that we come at such things as public issues from almost diametrically different backgrounds. There is something to be said for both perspectives though neither of us will ever see the world as does the other. A relationship is not diminished by the sharing of significant information. Instead, it is enhanced in the only way that human friendship can be: by allowing ever more complete access to the depths of one's being. Of this process both friends are the beneficiaries. The revealer becomes better acquainted with him/herself by the act of articulation and the listener has his/her humanity enhanced by the privilege of access to another human life. For both, the isolation which is endemic in our society is overcome.

Before turning to some of the sociological factors which bear upon friendship it might be useful to be more explicit about what may be the quality most conducive to being a friend. It is difficult to put this clearly or succinctly but I have the sense that it is some combination of passion and self-mockery. By passion I mean the capacity to care about things and people external to oneself. It is this capacity which enables one not just to hear but to listen to all the things that comprise our world. Rachel Carson had this ability and it was her revealingly entitled book, *The Silent Spring*, which first alerted many of us to the damage being done to the environment by widespread and thoughtless use of insecticides. By failing to hear familiar sounds for which she listened, she heard danger signals to which others were deaf. How often we might hear from friends silent cries for help were we more able to listen.

By self-mockery I mean the ability not to absolutize one's passions. This is vital to all human relationships. We must care for things and people but must also realize that what we care for, and the way in which we care, is not absolute. It is neither absolute within us, however much we pretend otherwise, nor may we assume that others should feel the same. To be able to combine passion with an appreciation for the relative worth of the object of one's enthusiasm is the goal to be sought. Too often, one encounters passions without self-criticism. This may be preferable to apathy but the unmodified passion frequently leads to cynicism and despair. Was some such combination of unrestrained enthusiasm and eventual cynicism not central to the tragedy of Jonestown? Whether or not that is true, it is surely fair to wonder where the passionate headline grabbers of the '60's have gone. Had they had a measure of self-criticism they might not have retreated as far as most have into privitization.

It is one of the tragedies of modern American life, perhaps especially for men, that we seem to value the quantities of our acquaintances over the quality of our friendships. We appear to believe that it is more important to be on a first name basis with large numbers of people than to have a few friends with whom to be intimate. This was the tragedy of Willy Loman in Arthur Miller's play, *Death of a Salesman*. He was known to many on his route as "Willy" but there was nobody with whom he could share the simple fact that he was failing at his job. Lacking the reality check of friendship, Willy could only retreat further into fantasies. The family had no loving alternative to the network of lies in which all were trapped. We have cited Freud's observation that two things, love and work, protect our sanity: work because it engages us with the life-giving world outside ourselves; love because its ability to listen to others enables us to be more truthfully in touch with our inner life. On this interpretation Miller's play might have been entitled, Abundance of Aquaintances, Poverty of Friendship. There may have been something inherently demeaning about Willy's work but I suspect that the impoverishment of his life and death requires a deeper explanation. That he lacked friends because salesmanship distances people from themselves and from others makes more sense than a simple indictment of selling.

At the final curtain we are left to imagine whether or not anybody benefitted from Willy's suicide. Within his family this did not seem likely. What we can say with certainty is that many people in mid-life have been brought to their senses about friendship by some dramatic events. For me it was, in part, the deaths I mentioned before. On one level I experienced the loss of a parent and friends through whom I had come to know myself, and on another level I experienced the indictment of a life which had too often sacrificed the claims of friendship to the demands of work.

Many people—traditionally men but increasingly women— are over-committed to work. It is from this over-commitment that springs the mid-life awareness of personal impoverishment. There are deprivations for which no income will compensate and the most grievous of these are in the broad area of human relationships. Is it surprising that many who have been work compulsives for twenty years begin to wonder about rectifying an imbalance? This is often a peculiarly urgent problem for those who have been most successful. Only certain qualities are relevant to the pursuit of success. There is no place for weakness; but who is endlessly strong? There is no place for ambivalence

but who is always single-minded? There is no place for compassion but who is uniformly ruthless? Only those qualities are
honored which establish one's superiority over others, one's
refusal to back down or concede anything. Some people really
believe that these are the ingredients of a successful life. Others
pretend such belief but have no relationships in which to
acknowledge otherwise. The true believer is the most socially
dangerous but the pretender may be hopelessly trapped. For as
long as s/he remains in the system there is no alternative to
self-isolating pretense. It is at this point that we see the hope and
risk of mid-life: a person may be able to ask, perhaps for the last
time, whether or not to perpetuate the pretenses. The possibility
that one will be able to ask the question is clearly enhanced if one
has a friend with whom such issues can be broached. The
prospects improve to the extent that, over the years, one has not
utterly concealed from others a capacity for compassion,
ambivalence and weakness. The person at mid-life who is
somewhat in touch with his/her foibles often finds the courage to
recognize the deprivations which have resulted from the
pretenses of strength.

It should be noted that there are two social factors which make
friendships difficult to sustain today: our high mobility and the
high incidence of divorce. While there was some family mobility
prior to World War II, in the decades since 1945 it has both
accelerated and included ever more of the population. The
heated undergraduate bull sessions in which I engaged
thirty-five years ago after an economics class have become
reality for millions of Americans annually. Then we disputed
the desirability of moving people to available jobs rather than
trying to maintain employment in population centers; today
prospering families may have moved half a dozen times between
a child's entrance and graduation from public schools. We, as
the children of post World War I, largely lived in one town, often
in but one house, all of our lives. The only itinerants we knew
were the Okies to whom Steinbeck introduced us. Today it is
often the privileged, or those in the process of becoming such,
who are the most highly mobile. They are not fleeing from Dust
Bowl farms to a California which doesn't want them. They are

moving from one green suburb to an identical neighborhood hundreds or thousands of miles away.

For young people the consequences of these patterns for friendships are momentous. I have known many students whose families were so mobile that they never established any meaningful childhood or adolescent friendships. Encouraged to concentrate on schoolwork, they arrived at college as intelligent and often cultured young men and women. It was as freshmen that they had their first opportunity to make and sustain friendships. Ventures which should have been launched much earlier, such as same-sex friendships and heterosexual relationships, were simply more difficult to undertake at eighteen than would have been the case earlier. The stakes are higher when one seeks initial friendships in one's late teens; it is a difficult time to learn that most people survive their social failures. Experienced early and often enough, and in the context of supportive family and friends, failure in peer relationships becomes part of one's acquired wisdom. The knowledge that wounds do heal becomes part of the identity one is fashioning. To know both success and failure in friendship during the adolescent years is crucial experience for fashioning a viable adulthood. To fail late may not be to fail safe.

Adults whose lives were formed in less mobile times or places may suffer less than their more vulnerable children but their problems with friendship are real. It is the exceptional family—though I have known them—which is able throughout high mobility to continue to put down roots upon arrival in a new community. This is an aptitude which those could wish for more who are unavoidably itinerant. More typical are those families who move in and move on, leaving little evidence that they had ever been. One hears them say such things as, "Oh, it's too painful trying to establish relationships when we know now we're only temporarily here. We did that for our first couple of moves and all we got was heartache. Now we're holding off on those things till retirement." The desire to protect oneself is understandable but I question that the effort to make friends could ever yield only heartache. Either no friendships were made and one departed with impunity or there were friendships which rewarded as well as saddened. Increasing numbers of families, unwilling to postpone indefinitely the rewards of friendship, decide against mobility and promotions. It may not be in the best interests of the multi-nationals but it says something about the importance of friendship and of the price that some are willing to pay to have the conditions in which its nurture is more likely.

The impact of divorce on friendships is more complex than is the fact of moving away. When a family leaves town they do remain intact and, while the situation has changed more than anybody acknowledges at the time of departure, there is the continuing possibility of maintaining aspects of the relationship by letters, phone calls, and occasional time shared. I recall the pleasure of a surprise visit from close friends who had moved to a part of the country in which we happened to be taking our twenty-fifth wedding anniversary trip. Little had changed in either of our lives to make it difficult to pick up more or less where we'd left off.

Divorce has a greater consequence for friendship. The couple may remain in town but the situation is utterly changed. People who have remained friends of the troubled couple through the tumultuous months and years which often precede a divorce confront a wholly new situation with the separation. With varying degrees of explicitness the former spouses may seek to keep the friends exclusively to themselves, seeking sympathy for their side of the former conflict. The friends, desiring to pass no judgments as to who was most at fault in the dissolved marriage and wishing to remain friends of both the former partners, must create a new relationship with both parties. This is often more complicated than it would be to initiate an acquaintance with a previously unknown single person. In this instance there would be no complicating common history, but with the former spouses it is otherwise. One must learn to befriend them as individual people whereas one knew them before only as a partner. I am not suggesting that this is an impossible assignment, just that it is impossible to unlearn all that one has known and valued about two people of a now dissolved relationship. In some ways it is easier to relate as a friend to the surviving widow or widower of a couple who were one's friends. For one thing, almost from the outset it is possible to speak of the deceased. There is a continuity of affection which, despite the death, makes it possible to relate to the survivor in a less dramatically changed way than to either of the divorced people. I am simply observing that divorce may alter the relationship of friends more dramatically than either the moving away of friends or the death of one of the partners who were one's friends. Perhaps there is something inherently threatening about divorce to every couple. After all, it does represent the failure of a particular friendship and the dissolution of an intimate relationship which had already survived both pleasure and pain. Since similar stabilities and instabilities are present in all relationships, the failure of any marriage is both a mystery and something of a threat. How do people reach a point where they are able to abandon all hope for a relationship which once was the source of their hope? No friendship or marriage is so solid, or so insensitive, as to be impervious to the tremors generated by the dissolution of another marriage to which one has been close.

I now turn from the loss of friends by other means to the death in mid-life of one of the close friends of my adulthood. I met Bob, several years my senior, in graduate school and formed a close friendship with him. In part I was taken by the breadth of his experience; he had worked closely for years with a major figure in American political life, owned a vast library and was well-read in areas with which I was limitedly familiar, and he had travelled widely. He became the mentor I needed. I read much at his suggestion and appreciated his willingness to let me struggle to articulate the ideas to which he introduced me. We may never have been intellectual equals; certainly we were not in the first years of our friendship.

The young woman who was to become my wife also liked him. He had interests and skills which I lacked—he was both a lover of the arts and a fine cook—and he welcomed us on frequent visits to his home. His appreciation for good kitchen tools and his ability at interior decoration, neither of which interested me then, were among the areas in which they enjoyed a mutually satisfying rapport. And we all liked books. In those days it was pleasant for the three of us to spend an evening moving from one second-hand bookshop to another, talking in changing pairs or together, perhaps buying a book or two (that was a time when a long-sought hardbound treasure might be had for a dollar!) and concluding our time together over cappucino. He was the older brother whom neither my wife nor I had had.

For over two decades he remained a close friend of our family, visiting occasionally, being a kindly "uncle" to our children, continuing to share with us the tribulations and the occasional successes of his peripatetic life. On one of these visits he reported that he was a homosexual. It is surprising that he had not previously acknowledged this since both my wife and I had long been aware of it. The disclosure in no significant way changed our relationship with him.

It was his excessive drinking that eventually became the crucial issue of our friendship. It was destroying his great potential and there was little that I or any of his friends were able to do. I had many painful calls from him in which the sadness and frustrations of his life often ended in uncontrollable tears, and I had probably as many calls from his landlord asking me to do something lest Bob burn down the apartment while drunk. On the occasions when I visited him he was able to maintain the appearance of sobriety and well-being, though occasionally there were outbursts of rage directed against those colleagues who he felt were undermining his work. A creative and imaginative person, he was forced by his limitations to be dependent on others who probably understood his plans and dreams only in part. They also had the ability to make necessary compromises which he too often viewed as betrayals.

The final years of his life were tragic. He suffered increasing paranoia, alcoholism, unemployment, indebtedness. Approximately a year prior to his death a group of his friends gathered from far parts of the country to consider what we might do for him. Despite the fact that considerable money was gathered from that group and from others, that arrangements were made for temporary hospitalization and therapy, that a respectable job was found for him in another city, I shall never be sure that these acts of friendship were not the worst thing we could have done. Bob was dead in less than a year.

For many reasons his death was one of the traumas of my mid-life. My affection for and indebtedness to him were great.

He had been the source of much encouragement and almost constant stimulation for years. I knew that he had my best interest at heart. He was, until near the end of his life, a joy to be with. I assume that he would have said some of the same things about me and my family. As one must, I grew beyond my need for him as a mentor but never beyond my need for him as a friend.

Yet I was ultimately unable to help him. Unable to acknowledge his own contributions to the difficulties of his work life, he increasingly blamed others for failures which were partly his own making. He simply could not be helped to see the ways in which he created problems for colleagues and for himself. Never fully understanding that there were many who liked and admired him without sharing his homosexuality, he never really accepted the fact of his particular sexual preference. Often urging others to accept themselves, he was unable to take his own good advice.

My trauma would seem to have had at least two major causes; the death of a dear friend and the realization of my inability to help avert that death. That he was determined to die now seems clear to me; that the council of friends may have helped to accomplish that, while intending the opposite, is an enduring suspicion. Enhanced appreciation for a good, if deeply flawed friend, and the recognition of my limitations were the gains of a friendship which was terminated by a premature death. And it took me almost a decade to be able to see their importance.

Many people have noted the traumatic effect of the death of one's parents. By their deaths the mid-life person is forced to recognize the fact of his/her own aging. In one's family one thereby becomes the senior person, the one to whom others may be inclined to turn. A much milder version of this is often experienced upon returning for one's final college year when all of the more experienced have graduated. Overnight, as it were, the senior becomes the person beyond whom there are no older ones. This change of status because of the absence of others who are older can be disturbing.

A common enough experience, it is not always easily embraced. As children of whatever age we were able to feel a sense of continuity, and avoid responsibility if so inclined, by being in the presence of elders. There was always somebody to whom we could turn whom we knew loved us and, although we didn't always take their advice, had our interests at heart. If we desired such from them, they were sources of information about family life before our birth and helped to recall events in our early lives. To have parents is to have access to both nurture and endlessly important information. To lose one's parents is to be left with memories and the opportunity to learn a new role in the life cycle. One must become within what one has become in fact, an elder in one's family.

The death of parents takes our discussion beyond the point where we began the second chapter. There we recognized the double bind in which persons in mid-life often find themselves when caught between the claims of both parents and children. With the death of one's parents that combination of responsibilities ceases only to be replaced by the new one of being a family elder. Since this is a unique role, involving considerable internal readjustment, we shall consider it as the mid-life search for roots. Along with the renewed interest in friendship, it is the means by which many people in mid-life begin to supplement or to replace identities which have been long defined largely by functional roles. It may become as important at this time to know more about the family of which one is now the head as it is to be the head of one's company or organization. Such has been part of my experience since my mother's death a decade ago and I want to suggest what it means to search for roots through memories of one's parents.

Since my parents were Scots immigrants I had little opportunity to know either set of grandparents. From my mother I learned about an affectionate and devout grandfather whose interests coincided with my own as an adolescent only to the extent that he enjoyed bowling. It was thirty years before I learned the difference between his activity on the green and my own! I did have a clan of relatives who lived in nearby cities and part of the joy of childhood was to visit them on holidays. It was on such occasions that I belonged to a larger family, which included its own somewhat distinctive language, humor, affection, and even foods. In our Yankee neighborhood my parents were somewhat distinctive because they never lost their accents and therefore it was reassuring to be with these relatives who spoke as they did and had many memories in common which they were usually willing to share with children who were not from the old country.

One of the important distinctions, which I learned to make early on, was between the "feel" of these family households. The fact that they were all related did not mean that the internal dynamics were similar. There were homes in which one could not be too careful about one's behavior, others which were more permissive as to what children could do. Although they all had approximately the same limited incomes, they differed in both generosity and in imaginativeness. Most were merry places though one was physically and emotionally darker. It was not till long after these aunts and uncles were dead that I came to see an enduringly important distinction between them: some were what I have come to call life givers, and others were more life withholders. While the ability to apply the labels came long after my childhood experience, I suspect that I early realized that there were some families where I simply knew that I was welcomed. On the other hand, at least one uncle and aunt always suggested that there was something more I had to become before they could approve of me. Needless to say, I never succeeded with the latter and progressively saw less of them. They withheld what children look for from others who are important to their lives.

Before attempting to draw out the significances of such memories for people at mid-life, let me report an event which occurred at about age fifty. Our grown daughter had come home for a few days and we were talking on the porch over coffee at twilight. I remember the time of day because in Minnesota there is often a condition of summer light before dusk by which I am peculiarly moved. By a series of questions she had me telling her about these relatives, few of whom she had ever known. As I spoke of one particular aunt and uncle I began to sob. Since they were long dead this could not have been simply an instance of delayed grief. The best I could make of it was that this particular couple were the most consistent of the life givers and I was saddened to realize that they could never do for her what they had often done for me. I suspect that I wondered also whether I had been comparably life-giving in my relationships with my children and with all youth.

Whatever the full explanation of my tears may be, this was an occasion in which I saw something important about the nature of my own roots which may be true for everybody. One's legacy is mixed and it is each person's responsibility to make the best possible use of what actually has been received. So much of the current curiosity about family origins is mere antiquarianism. There is little to be gained from charting a geneology. The point is, after decades of attempting to live as though functional roles defined one, one should become acquainted with the actual, conflicting people by whom one's early life was shaped. Here are the sources of our generosity, our fears, our gifts and our disabilities. Here is the mixed bag from which we yet have opportunity to make a life more characterized by integrity than by despair.

I consider the realization of the mixed bag of one's past fortunate. If we had identical parents there would be no discussion, we would simply replicate them. That they were not identical begins with the fact that one was female, the other male. Since it was their behavior as well as their genes by which we were shaped we have some options as to what we will make of what they produced. Not everything is open to us, any more than it was possible to replicate them, but a range of possibilities does exist. Gradually it is we who decide how to combine ingredients in our personal legacy to fashion our lives. The importance of this task is most clearly seen by recognizing that it is every person's responsibility to fashion a whole life out of elements which parents were never able to reconcile. I, for example, have had to seek ways to synthesize into one credible manhood my father's vision of a better society which was rooted in his Fabian trade-unionism and my mother's desire for self-improvement which grew out of her individualistic Scots' piety.

Long suspicious of the church as an ally of the oppressing class, my father had little sympathy for my mother's pietism. He did, however respect her as a person and later in life occasionally accompanied her to church. The conflict between their understanding of the sources of evil—his emphasis on corporate or structural factors, hers on personal behavior—was never resolved in their common life. It is part of my burden and excitement to synthesize, or at least to hold together meaningfully, such disparate convictions. I believe this to be the good fortune of our humanity: that our lives are neither predetermined nor utterly free. There are many givens from the past but each person bears the human burden by doing distinctively what s/he can with what has been received. It may be that each person does no more than to reshuffle these givens. To put it this way, however, diminishes the importance of even the most modest exercise of personal freedom and creativity. Not everything is possible for everybody; only some things are. What we make of these givens is what is decisive for the shape of our lives. For me this involves integrating my father's understandings of the importance of societal factors and my mother's emphasis on the personal. The process remains incomplete.

While there is a basic givenness to a personality, an enduring continuity which began taking shape long before the adolescent's identity crisis, the actual ways in which many of these disparate elements are related to each other vary from day to day. Despite our reasonable expectation of personal consistency this is only true to a relative degree. Circumstances change, time passes; it is not possible to be indifferent to these. The parent who was once a tower of strength may become a helpless invalid. The infant once utterly dependent becomes increasingly strong and self-reliant. Never are we free from the awesome privilege of drawing appropriately from the diverse treasures of our family legacy to deal with ever new situations. What is needed, and what mid-life may make possible, is a reacquaintance with some of the diverse elements of one's past. Such self-awareness both makes for the resiliency which modern life requires and frees one from some of the rigidity which is dysfunctional in both personal and professional life.

The great promise which mid-life holds is precisely this: that, as the result of many universal and culture-specific factors which we identified earlier, a person may be more disposed to get back in touch with more of him/herself than has been possible for decades. The possibility for fashioning a somewhat new life for oneself really does exist, and the resources for the task lie in the long-neglected diversity of memories and capabilities. The polarities within us—the male/female duality, the capacity for solitude and gregariousness, the dependency/independency—long suppressed for the sake of functional roles may be re-embraced. There may be no greater or later potential for enhancing one's own life or of enriching the lives of all those whom one's life touches. By drawing upon the memories which the death of a parent evokes we may discover the exciting and frightening prospects of the middle years.

The person who is increasingly in touch with the diversity of his/her past is in the process of becoming a senior. It is not just the passage of time which so qualifies one. We all know many people at and beyond mid-life who either desperately pretend a youthfulness they no longer possess or who have refused the self-acquaintance which experience might have provided. Neither of these two has the resiliency of those who are profiting from mid-life. It is pretense which precludes the resiliency: the attempt to deny the passage of time, to ignore the complexity of one's actual life. It really is truth which liberates. Every pretense, and every dishonesty, requires energy to maintain the concealment and makes it that much more difficult for others to reach us. The misuse of energy is fatiguing and results only in the diminution of the satisfaction of lives in touch with each other. Pretense keeps all at a distance: the pretender from him/herself, which is the ultimate source of despair; the pretender from all others, which makes so much social life lacking in nourishment.

Persons progressively free from pretense are neither threatened by self-acquaintance nor inaccessible. They relish what they know of their imperfection and are able to help others come to terms with themselves. Truly, they are life-givers because they have affirmed their own lives. Connected by organic ties with their past, they are free to draw upon their diverse resources for the sake of the future. Familiar with their particular story and nourished by it, they are not trapped in it. The story itself—the distinctive mother and father, the variety of relatives, the host of associations and experiences—is itself so varied that entrapment is impossible.

Of my half dozen uncles only one spoke often and adamantly of his determination never to return to Scotland. Of all these men only he strongly resisted the desire often expressed by my other relatives for a trip back home. He not only resisted the idea, he ridiculed it. Yet, it is an interesting fact, that of all those relatives only he is buried there. All the others acknowledged affection for the place of their birth but, at least for the men, felt that they never could afford so to indulge themselves. Upon his retirement and the death of his wife he had returned to Scotland. Clearly out of touch with his own story he was a pretender, a life-withholder. He grew old but nobody benefited from having had contact with him.

We began this chapter with the report of an important, unanticipated experience which I had while with a group of students for a mid-winter conference. Reflections on the three people who were called to mind that afternoon put me in closer touch with important threads in my own story. Inherently rewarding as I believe this process to be, we should note that it is rarely completely pleasant, because of illusions one often has to discard. It is also difficult because we have often distanced ourselves from people and events important to our story. Sometimes, however, it may be surprising, as the following suggests.

Several years ago I received an invitation to attend a conference in Jerusalem. Since I was interested in the topic and had never been in Israel I accepted the invitation. My acceptance was influenced by the inclusion of three days in Athens on the way home. Having spent several weeks in Greece a decade earlier I was convinced that, whatever the value of the Jerusalem conference, the trip would be worthwhile because of the opportunity for a brief return to Greece. For a host of reasons, including my interest in Greek philosophy and theatre, I was convinced that Greece was intrinsic to my story. It is difficult for a longtime member of the academic community not to believe that the cradle of Western Civilization is also the cradle in which s/he was deeply nurtured. So, carefully planning how I would be able to make the most of the precious hours in Athens, I boarded the El Al flight at Kennedy Airport. Hours later I was awakened during our approach to the Ben Gurion Airport at Tel Aviv by a recording of "Hava Nagilla." The air cooled and cleared as our bus proceeded from sea level up to our Jerusalem hotel. Had the conference been my only experience I would have been strongly stimulated because of the use made of sites in the Old City for our study of space and architecture. There is an inescapable sense of history at such places as the Western Wall, the Dome of the Rock within the ancient Temple Mount, and the Church of the Holy Sepulchre. Each of these places—respectively important to Jew, Moslem, and Christian, and within a short distance of each other—reminds one both of what is central to the three traditions and of the inherent potential for conflict in the Holy City.

Prior to the opening of the conference we had several day-long excursions to places of significance outside of Jerusalem. While neither Bethlehem nor Nazareth, especially the former, could be called anything other than commercialized, there were many strangely moving places: the well at Jericho, the partially rebuilt synagogue at Capernaum, Megiddo, the Sea of Galilee, Qumran, Masada. These sights were all central to the Hebrew Bible, the New Testament, and the intertestamental period. But, none was more moving to me than Masada where the nine hundred Jewish sectarians withstood Hadrian's army for two years from the fortress which the mad Herod had had built. A few hours before the Roman troops were to breach the walls the faithful community of Jews committed suicide as an expression of the freedom which they affirmed as Children of the Covenant. It was because of their faith that they refused to be demeaned.

These experiences were crucial for clarifying my understanding of my story. As the time approached for our departure I found myself doing things which could not have been foreseen as recently as a fortnight before. I was trying, unsuccessfully as it turned out, to find some way to avoid going to Greece in order to have the few extra hours in this land which had become so important to my self-understanding. The depths of my story are more informed by the Wailing Wall than by the Athenian Acropolis, more by the unlocatable Hill of the Skull than by the Delphic Oracle, more by the building stones hewn by slaves from Solomon's underground quarry near the Damascus Gate than by the Pentellic sculpture of the Elgin Marble. It is not a matter of the superiority of one over the other. The merits and demerits of Athens and Jerusalem will rightly be an endless topic for debate, often without recognizing that they address different aspects of human experience. The importance of the beautiful may never be completely reconcilable with an equally central emphasis on the useful. Both are capable of disastrous overemphasis but neither is dismissable. The matter is this: which of these traditions puts one in touch with the deepest levels of his/her story? Which evokes those people and events in one's own experience which most need to be recalled and reclaimed? Which tradition contributes most persuasively to that mid-life search for the organic ties of one's life? There is no single formula which will assure each person at mid-life the successful rediscovery of ignored roots. And therein is the glory and trial of mid-life. Each person's history is distinctive. No matter what we share with all people, we must come to grips with the resources of our own distinctive stories. The key to the potential for mid-life renewal lies within every particular story.

The point that I want to stress in conclusion is that because of the complexities of any individual's life, and because of the limits to what one may impose upon any single relationship, it is important to be able to give to and to draw from a variety of relationships. It is tempting to overburden marriage at this time of life, to expect one's spouse to be everything one needs. While I am deeply respectful of the capacity of a good marriage to enlarge the range of issues to which partners are sensitive, I am equally aware of the need to set limits to what one asks of another. For example, while my wife has been wonderfully responsive to my efforts over many years to become clearer about my own life, the fact is that friends, especially men who both shared some of my concerns and had a perspective which my wife couldn't have, have also been very important in helping mo to achieve greater clarity. One must recognize the importance of a number of relationships to accomplish the needed self-clarifications. I was helped on one occasion by hearing a group of young people singing the folk song, "I get by with a little help from my friends." I wanted to modify this helpful reminder of the human condition only by substituting for "a little" the words "a lot of!" That better described my experience.

Finally, let me offer a qualification about the title of this chapter, Relationships at Mid-life: Extra-marital. In my emphasis on relationships I have wanted to stress the utter importance

of continuing friendships for achieving the self-understanding
which people seek at mid-life. Fleeting relationships have
limited usefulness in enabling us to become better acquainted
with ourselves precisely because they lack endurance. At best
they mute temporarily the mid-life imperative to self-acquaintance. The process of self-awareness is not just a matter of
becoming intellectually reacquainted with forgotten or neglected aspects of one's story. This, to put it too simply, would be the
Greek temptation: to assume that, difficult as this may be, it is
sufficient to know oneself. Unlike the individualism which
underlies the Oracle's exhortation, the Jerusalem tradition
seems to me wiser. It recognizes the inherent relatedness of
human lives and it is this recognition which undergirds all that I
have tried to say about marriage and extra-marital relationships.
It is in the context of these continuing friendships that
self-knowledge may come and it is within these relationships
that one must learn to act on the consequences of that acquired
knowledge. Those who listen must do so painstakingly even
when they do not understand. Like a good parent we must learn
to live with the clumsy and sometimes hurtful efforts of the
mid-life adolescent who is trying to learn to act from a new and
precarious center of self-understanding. Those who are being
helped must learn both to trust the other and to relinquish
illusions which may no longer be determinative of one's
behavior. Growth is never assured; the only assurance is that, at
best, it takes time. There is a shared grief as each illusion is
identified and, reluctantly and slowly, released. There is, if you
will, an ongoing experience of death. But this, I believe, is the
precondition of any rebirth. So understood, we may grasp more
clearly why Jung observed that the heart of the problems
presented by his mid-life patients was inherently religious.

While the mention of religion is premature, it is necessary
before concluding the present discussion to be clear about one
matter. It is not just at mid-life and in the aging process that
people's capacity for being religious is enhanced. It may be
tempting to equate the mid-life tendency to look inward with
religion. Is it not the case in our society that this time of life is, for
many, the first opportunity to pay attention to other than the
external aspects of one's life? If this is the only viable timetable

for many people then the most must be made of it, for it is the wholeness of lives which is at stake.

My problem arises with the tendency to identify the inward movement of lives as itself the primary goal of religion. In my understanding that is but a part, albeit a crucial part, in one's religious maturation. The goal is a new relationship to the external world and though there have been and will be many such efforts to confine the concerns of religious faith to inward reform, they are doomed. However difficult it is to find the balance between the within and the without we may never obscure the fact that we need the world for friendships, for work, for creativity. It is of the world that we are made, by its fruits that we are sustained; it is the source of our sanity and of our anguish.

Temporary emphasis on one's internal development may be healthy compensation. There is often long neglect of the inner life to be overcome. But the inner life by itself is no safer refuge than was a fully externalized existence. The task is to relate them in such a way that they inform, correct, nourish and strengthen each other. Their relationship is inherently dialectical: the world producing tasks to be undertaken as the result of inward struggle; the inner life bringing fresh perspective to bear upon and to modify the agenda on which the world insists. It is an endless, two-way street requiring the ability to look both ways, almost simultaneously. Probably my most important task as a teacher in a liberal arts college is to help students to realize that the learning process involves much more than the mastery of material. It requires one to let the material have its unsettling effects upon one's inner life. The process is always two-way: to grasp our forebears' understanding of reality, in which process the student may be master; to allow that encounter with others to make a difference in our lives, wherein the student is subject.

This work of a liberal education describes my experience during a decade of mid-life. I have been becoming familiar with realities which I once thought were and could be kept external to me. Friendships which were terminated by death and the death of a parent have proven impossible to ignore. By reflecting on a number of relationships which had been important to me, I found the direction of my life slightly changing. I came to see that this information about which I had previously been quite casual enabled me to gain a measure of control over my present life. I did not need to be defined by my roles. The ability to be fully in but not of any particular world was the mid-life gift of certain relationships. Like a student, I discovered that the mastery of certain materials made a world of difference to my inner life and the direction of my future.

It is this gift, which we may begin to receive in mid-life, which will be fully given to those who will be intentional about their aging. That we did not make our lives but are responsible for them; that there is more to us than meets the eye or ear; that we are sustained by the world and want future generations to be able to be so sustained: these are among the incipient awarenesses of the middle years which may come to sharp focus and power as we age.

CHAPTER 7

In Praise of Aging

It is the primary intent of this chapter to be a statement in praise of aging. This will appear gratuitous only to those unable to recognize the widespread American antipathy toward growing older. Given the inevitability of the aging process, whatever the medical prospects for life-extension, our aversion is at least wrong-headed.

It is not my intent, however, to argue for the obvious fact that we are all aging. Rather, I shall contend that growing older involves distinctive opportunity for growth. If this opportunity should be thwarted, as it is for many in our society, the consequences are universally bad. Older people are denied access to important tasks appropriate to their stage of life. Equally important and equally undervalued are the consequences of this denial for the rest of society. If elders are not encouraged to deal with their proper agenda, the rest of us are cut off from understandings which only they can acquire and provide.

Thus, we shall search for the wisdom long thought to be a mark of older persons. We will not necessarily look to those elders who remain active or wish to be productive, though neither of these need be discouraged. The trouble with activity and productivity is that, in the main, they represent behavior appropriate to earlier stages of life. Some elders will continue to be active and productive but this ability should not be made the major criterion for positive attitudes toward them. Aging's beauty is to be seen in the way some older individuals relate to themselves and to the outside world. While it is theoretically possible for younger people to have such beauty, this is unlikely both because of their preoccupation with tasks appropriate to earlier stages of life and because of societal biases against aging.

Since my appreciation for the life cycle was nurtured by the writings of Erik H. Erikson, and because it is important for our approach to aging to recognize the dynamics of the stages through which we pass, we shall first summarize briefly some of the crucial assumptions which undergird his description of normal human development. We are particularly interested in those understandings which bear upon the process of growing older.

The extent to which an older person is able to affirm the integrity of his/her life, rather than to despair of it, will be largely determined by the adequacy of earlier maturation. Whether an elder perceives beauty, or is primarily disgusted by life's ugliness, is not an achievement of the final years. Since there is beauty and ugliness in all lives at all of the stages the task is to be able to affirm one's God-given beauty without having to conceal the rest. At no stage are we either as beautiful or as ugly as we sometimes think. With eyes open to the enduring "mix" of our lives we need to be able to affirm both the givens and our potential for growth at all times. What Galway Kinnell has to say about self-blessing in the following poem can just as easily apply to old people.

> The bud
> stands for all things,
> even for those things that don't flower,
> for everything flowers, from within, of self-blessing;
> though sometimes it is necessary
> to reteach a thing its loveliness,
> to put a hand on its brow
> of the flower
> and retell it in words and in touch
> it is lovely
> until it flowers again from within, of self-blessing;
> as Saint Francis

put his hand on the creased forehead
of the sow, and told her in words and in touch
blessings of earth on the sow, and the sow
began remembering all down her thick length,
from the earthen snout all the way
through the fodder and slops to the spiritual curl of the tail,
from the hard spininess spiked out from the spine
down through the great broken heart
to the blue milken dreaminess spurting and shuddering
from the fourteen teats into the fourteen months sucking
    and blowing beneath them:
the long, perfect loveliness of sow.[1]

Given the aversions of our society there is no time when that ability to affirm the "long, perfect loveliness of sow" is more difficult or more urgent than in life's evening.

In the second section of this chapter I propose a theological rationale in support of the developmental understanding of lives. While there is an important sense in which successful passage through the life stages is not the key to Christian self-understanding, (see Galatians 3:28) I contend both that these stages are the ordinary school in which lessons of growth are to be learned and that they may be transcended only as they are completed. This discussion includes the following: the importance of the whole life-cycle; the peril of fantasy-inspired efforts to break out of it; two functions of Christian faith regarding the tensions inherent in the life-cycle; and, finally, the description of related developments which make aging beautiful.

Taking my cue from another poet, I want to contend that Browning was right in 'Rabbi Ben Ezra" despite virtually uniform opinion to the contrary, "The best is yet to be,/The last of life for which the first was made." Even a decade ago I couldn't have imagined myself saying such a thing.

As we turn to the more original portion of this chapter it may be helpful to underscore several matters. First, while there are accompanying outer realities, struggles of the life-stages are primarily internal. Thus, in human development, meaning is less to be associated with external events like birthdays and anniversaries, paychecks and bank accounts, academic degrees and publications, than with internal workings and re-workings of the normal agenda of the life-cycle. This fact creates deep problems for a society which, having tried to confine the sources of meaning to external accomplishments, has limited ability to encourage accomplishments which are primarily invisible. Appreciation for those qualities which allowed our economy to grow rapidly from the mid-nineteenth century led us to believe we were opening up new possibilities for human development, when in fact we were simply transferring ever greater portions of the burden of providing meaning to our lives from internal to external factors. To the extent that these external emphases are also rigidly normative they thwart the human fact of growing older and the need for faith in aging. Along with other institutions, religion must provide a basis for defence of internal development.

Second, the life stages involve endless tensions arising from the need for both continuity and change. As we shall see shortly, this tension is often experienced most vividly in both adolescence and mid-life, the latter being something of a recurrence of the former. But at virtually all times there is a potentially creative tension between habit and the desire for novelty. In Christian history we see this in terms of the emphases in different periods on tradition and the spirit. While one or the other may be dominant, both are intrinsic to human lives both institutionally and personally. Those who insist on either continuity or change, the adequacy of tradition or the animation of the spirit, betray fundamental lack of faith. I believe that it is through the endless tension between continuity and change that God works to fashion in us that faith in ourselves which enables us to affirm challenges otherwise avoided. The process of aging appears to be the last chance.

Third, nobody is beyond further growth. No person ever reaches a stage where further development is either inappropriate or unwanted. We all need and wish to keep growing, though there is legitimate resting and "normal" arrested times. (Seen this way, the sin of the Pharisees which Jesus so vigorously exposed was the willful refusal to recognize any need for further growth.) Actually, we never lose the desire to develop further as persons. Evidence of this is seen in the therapeutic work of

Lawrence LeShan with terminally ill cancer patients. ("Mobilizing the Life Force," unpublished paper.) Fully aware of the irrelevance of counseling to their illness, most patients chose to participate in individual and group therapy. With enough time and the right approach everybody can have his/her desire for growth activated by somebody—and not necessarily some professional! (cf. Reuel Howe, *The Creative Years*, chapter 5, The Seabury Press, 1959.)

Fourth, the polar tensions in every stage are complementary rather than mutually exclusive. While at each stage the positive pole must predominate for healthy growth, the complementary pole persists appropriately in a minor role. Thus, trust must be fashioned in infancy as the primary response to reality but, since neither the world nor one's perceptions of it are fully trustworthy, some mistrust is both unavoidable and functional. It is never a matter of utterly obliterating the negative pole; rather, of assigning it its proper role in the totality of one's life.

Over the course of human development these polar identities are the agenda for each particular life-stage. While the healthy life cycle calls for dominance of a positive pole—i.e., trust, ego integrity—the complementary pole is never thoroughly eliminated. Thus mistrust, which becomes paranoia when dominant, is indeed a needed resource in a world which both is and is not trustworthy.

Finally, normal development from basic trust to ego integrity involves not only progressive self-discovery but an ever wider and deeper participation in the total human venture. This is dysfunctional in a society committed to the efficiency of specialization. Instead it represents an alternative to our exploitative way of relating to the external world. Since both our externalization of the sources of meaning and our preference for progressive narrowing of one's range of activity are inimical to the aging process we have the ingredients for serious conflict. The same society which hurried youth through adolescence also refuses passage from adulthood to a stage where producing and consuming become less important. This restrictiveness, which in undermining the distinctive tasks of the various life-stages denies the contributions which the generations have to make to each other, is another point at which Christian faith joins issue with prevailing societal assumptions and institutions. So powerful may social attitudes be in a given time and place that they may make it at least difficult for some and impossible for others to move on to the next, normative life-stage. Such refusal to embrace the distinctive contributions of the life-stages to each other may be both the strength of our economy and the gravest threat to our desire for human development.

While the Christian faith is not partial to any particular life stage it is committed to the defense of any imperilled stage. It takes this stance on the assumption that God is the source of meaning behind all of the stages, that God has set the life agenda in order that people's lives might be centered while they cope with the flux of human development. Augustine rightly noted that hearts are restless until they are centered in God. This, however, should not be used as a basis either for rejecting the life stages, which are endlessly changing, or for preserving Christian faith in only one mode. Human sensibilities vary with one's stage of life: the adolescent is responsive to God in ways distinct from those of his/her grandparent. Thus, the Good News must be so fashioned that its goodness may be heard by those at all stages. While all people have some ability to empathize with others we are equally obliged to pay attention to what God may be trying to accomplish in us where we are. It is the refusal to affirm one's present tasks that leads to inhumanity toward others. There is no basis for the sense of kinship from which humane acts come. The generality of the temptation to ignore one's own current issues or to prefer to deal with somebody else's agenda should not conceal the fact that it is only the content, not the presence, of the temptation, which varies with one's location in the life cycle.

To me this is self-evident. It is not, however, widely acknowledged. It seems to encourage a self-preoccupation long condemned as un-Christian. To be able to distinguish between selfishness and self-love, however, is crucial. Selfishness which deserves as much pity as condemnation, is the plight of those incapable of self-love. The ability to distinguish between self-centeredness and the desire to pay attention to the issues appropriate to one's life is crucial to my argument. Could it be that a society which both hurries the young through childhood and adolescence and refuses to encourage people to take on the proper work of aging encourages the very self-centeredness which it then condemns? Increasingly I suspect this to be the case: that we cultivate selfishness by our inability to honor the normative agenda of the distinct life stages. Can we with impunity rush ourselves through or past the inner growths to be accomplished by everyone? If Erich Fromm is right in his discussion of these matters, self-love is the antithesis of selfishness.[2] It seems to me that a proper self-love, to which Scripture exhorts us, means paying loving attention to those agendas which come forth, from God, as one's life unfolds. To make the believer capable of such attention, while sin urges neglect, is a primary function of Christian faith.

Whether or not religious faith is true lies beyond our present scope. Whether or not there is a referent with which faith is connected is obviously crucial, but the question of God's existence cannot be answered under any conditions simply with a yes or no. What we should try to do is to be clearer about the issues to which faith in God is one possible response. The alternatives to faith, once the life-issues are clearly seen, include stoicism, despair, and fantasy. The point I stress is that both faith and non-faith are related to the important growth accomplished between birth and death. I emphasize this because: 1) faith is often presented as a device for avoiding such painful struggle; 2) properly understood, faith may be the better resource for affirming the growth which we would often rather avoid. I say this out of the conviction that God's agenda for us is literally endless. In one sense faith is the ability to remain endlessly open to new possibility. Since God's communication with people has always been understood to be indirect, I propose that it is mediated through the demands for growth presented in every life-stage.

Since fantasy, which is in some ways akin to faith, rejects such slow growth we must look at it more closely. Early in the first act of Marlowe's play, Dr. Faustus asks this question: "Shall I have the spirits resolve me of all ambiguity?" This flight was anticipated in his earlier suggestion that all human achievements, most of which he had mastered, were "paltry." While we have probably all despaired of human effort, especially our own, the Faustian desire to transcend all limitations is not an illustration of faith but is its antithesis. Faith may not be convincing but it is never free to abandon the immediate tasks whether these involve personal development or social change. As we shall try to show, rarely are the personal and social tasks unrelated.

I was helped to see the significance of Faustus' question during a production at the Tyrone Guthrie Theater in Minneapolis. In this interpretation by Ken Ruta the resolution of all ambiguity, for which Faustus traded his soul, resulted in his loss of contact with all ordinary reality. The superhuman powers which he thought he had acquired by his bargain with Mephistopheles were illusions made credible to him by the connivance of his mocking acquaintances. Faustus was mad and others mocked him by pretending the reality of his illusions. With this interpretation I understood Marlowe to be saying something germane to my argument: short of insanity, there is no escape from ambiguity.

Another illustration of the perils of fantasy is to be found in Hannah Greene's autobiographical/fictional report of her psychosis, *I Never Promised You a Rose Garden*. Finding her life as a child insufficiently rewarding she fantasized a world of spirits to which she retreated for solace. In the course of time, however, the creatures took on a life of their own, did not wait to be called, and became progressively harmful. Not only did the adolescent lack the resources to begin to fashion a viable identity, but the spirits which she had fantasized for her comfort progressively forced a retreat from adulthood to ever more self-destructive infancy.

There are no instant rose gardens, no quick resolution of life's mixture of good and evil, pleasure and the unpleasant. Unlike Doctor Faustus, however, Hannah had a friend and therapist who refused either to accept her fantasies or to abandon her. Unable to resolve every ambiguity, the doctor offered only the care by which the slow, painful reconstruction of a life was possible. Such attention to the ordinary is the work of love, which heals by its patient commitment to the truth.

The life of faith involves the reality-check of other people to keep us from becoming captive to our private fantasies. Faith is not inimical to imagination, since we have no other personal resource by which to sense the possibility of growth beyond the present. But such growth must be publicly corroborative and only has to do with the next step which we must take rather than the tasks of which we may be capable a year or a decade hence. Fantasy's giant stride involves the danger of destructive steps backward in the name of moving rapidly ahead. Both Faustus and Hannah Greene so fantasized as to be threatened by self-destruction. He lost his soul and she barely found a way out of the torture of wild fantasy. Fantasy would sacrifice the possible (paltriness) to the desirable (total transcendence). Faith would enable us to embrace the possible as the desirable.

Historically, faith has meant many things. The meaning I wish to emphasize with regard to aging is this: that trust in God results in trust in self. In faith we learn to respect the agenda which arises within us at the stages of life. It is by affirming God as the source of meaning within the life cycle that we may be empowered to affirm the endless demands for development from birth to death.

These assertions assume that the life stages are God's ordinary schoolhouse for instructing us in matters intrinsic to our humanity. While there are infinite variations on healthy adaptations to the demands of all the stages, there is a normative development at each. The God-given assignment is to recognize the realities actually operative at any given time. It is because such knowledge is not automatic that we must think about the functions of faith. We need empowerment to enable us to move beyond today's adjustment to tomorrow's uncertainties. The resources for this growth are always present in our accumulated achievements but we are not naturally confident of that fact!

Faith empowers by causing us to embrace our internal ambiguities and at the same time resist the social pressures which would overly confine our lives. To see how faith accomplishes this we should first look to several everyday tensions, keeping in mind that they are suggestive rather than exhaustive: male/female, active/passive, faith/doubt. Each of these complementaries is present within everybody. As with Erikson's polarities, one may be dominant but the other should never be so suppressed as to be out of reach. To the extent that we suppress successfully there are at least two dangers: energy that could otherwise be used elsewhere is employed to maintain the concealment; and, more seriously, the suppressed reality has not been eliminated. Out of conscious control it must and will find some destructive means of expression.

To begin with, I assume an androgynous model of human sexuality. As the offspring of two parents each of us has both male and female genes. The particular balance of these components determines whether the child is a boy or a girl. Whatever the sex, the distinction is not absolute and must not be made so. The tendency to absolutize, however, is a temptation which the Christian faith must resist. Without trying to identify specifically masculine and feminine qualities, I am arguing importance of being able to draw upon the full range of our sexual potential. When we are alive to our complex sexuality we may become full human beings, children of God.

Secondly, I assume a universal capacity for both activity and non-activity. While personal patterns rarely conform these days we all still sleep and afterwards awake. Only the emphasis changes. The problem is that our society is partial to activity. Think of some of the cliches which reveal our attitude. "If you want something to get done, ask a busy person." Or, "Don't just stand there, do something!" Since I wish to affirm both activity and inactivity, I need a resource stronger than social pressure in order to be able to affirm inactivity as the complement to compulsive busyness. We need time for being not-active, for being passive, for reflection, for receiving, for being dependent, and it is a function of faith to resist every effort to evaluate lives primarily in terms of how busy they are.

By the way in which I have spoken of faith's functions it may seem that faith itself is free of ambiguity. If that is the case, as some insist, I do not find it confirmed in my experience. As a seemingly necessary leap for which there is only limited proof, faith unavoidably involves doubt. When discussing Erikson's stages we spoke of the experience of intimacy as a commitment to imperfection. Without this experience one holds back, preferring to await some perfect thing or person to give oneself to without fear of failure or compromise. Isn't the need for an unambiguous faith at least analogous to this? A doubt-free faith would be one where all elements of risk are removed. In it there would be no possibility of loss of self. Inasmuch as I recognize in this a desire to be free of responsibility for my life, to transcend the possibility of utter loss of self, I recognize the presence of Doctor Faustus. This helps me to remember that there are no spirits able to resolve me of all ambiguity, that nobody has promised me a rose garden, that I must live merely as a fully human person—as a child of God faithful and doubting.

However, to be children of God is not to be passive before society's narrow expectations but to insist upon the full spectrum of the life cycle and the persistence of the complementary polarities of each of the life stages. Faith engenders the capacity for defiance, as William Blake suggested when he characterized Christ as "Humble before God/Arrogant before men." Clearly, not all arrogance derives from humility before God. However, resistance to any societal threat to affirming the inherent ambiguities of human experience is Christian behavior. In our society aging is just such an imperilled stage and it is part of faith's function to defend this God-given work.

There are burdens inherent in the development of both faith and life. In both there is the temptation to avoid the challenges of growth. For some forms of faith there is the additional false burden of absolutizing: life's ambiguities must be transcended. For example, some hold that all that contradicts love must be eliminated. While life's goal is the enhancement of the capacity to love, I am equally convinced that love's opposites persist to the end. It is faith's work to free us to acknowledge the enduring ambivalences. Thus equipped, we are able to work at those particular improvements of which we may be capable. For the false burden of perfection we substitute the real burden of possible growth.

When resisting pressure which would overly confine our lives, the temptation is to take a radically anti-social stance. This may prove to be tactically necessary, but it is not the strategy to which I am basically inclined. Still, one must be vigilant in criticism of every status quo. There will always be some arrangement, born out of compromise, that will test the duty of faith to be responsive to all injustice. In the context of this book it is the implications of such arrangements for the aging that concern us. Perhaps it is easier to care for elderly people than for other oppressed groups because we can all feel the aging one within each of us. Nonetheless I suffer a great deal of uncertainty about the developmental soundness of many programs that have recently been directed toward the elderly.

Because we live in a society committed to production and consumption, a society primarily concerned with external assumptions about the sources of meaning, we are uncomfortable with aging. We are usually characterized as committed to a cult of youth and, if he had found those springs, our national saviour might have been St. Ponce. Obviously, there is some truth in the characterization. I wish to suggest, however, that we pretend more affection for youth than we intend. Our commitment is more to "adulthood" than to the turbulence of adolescence. Our zeal to move youth out of the uncertainties of their search for an identity and their fumblings for intimacy convinces me that to be young is not really our preference. We are a society with such a limited range of approved behavior that we are unwilling to let youth remain young and for the aging to grow old. Is it because both age groups are outsiders that youth and the aging often both feel a kinship for each other and an antipathy for adults?

Is it the vulnerability of both youth and age to major physical changes and uncertainty about the future to which adults are antipathetic? Certainly adolescence and aging pose radical questions, as do few other stages of life, about the meaningfulness of the busy lives to which adults are committed. It has occurred to me that many adults are really closet adolescents. I refer not to men and women who are obviously immature but to many who consider themselves to be grown up. Hurried through childhood and forced to pretend clarity about career intentions, they hide behind work-compulsion lest the inadequacy of their self-understanding and their commitment to their work be discovered. The openness of adolescent uncertainty about the future and the disturbing questions about the past which elders raise are equally threatening to the self-justifying activity of adults. Lucky are those sufficiently shaken by the traumas of mid-life to come out of the closet and acknowledge their uncertainties. They could discover that strength is not reduced by admitting weakness nor faith diminished by doubt.

Busyness may be the best way to characterize middle-class adulthood. There may be activities other than work, leisure for instance, but these are really justified in our minds either as further activity or as a means to better equip us for our primary form of busyness. Recreation time, weekends and vacations, are often maniacally busy. Were we still familiar with agricultural life we would know that there are seasons for busyness and productivity. Seeds must be planted, weeds eliminated, and produce harvested. But the old rhythm of intense work and inactivity no longer satisfies our need to be productive. We are enslaved to the machines which were to be our liberation! Few are able to justify unscheduled time. Children are endlessly urged to more activities and more intensive schooling, apparently on the assumption that these will better equip them for the appropriate adulthood which is their destiny. Parents who may not have found their busy lives particularly fulfilling unhesitatingly urge the same patterns onto their children. The hope seems to be that more of the same will do for children what it didn't do for their parents.

Damaging as this mania is to youth it is even more cruel to elders. It denies them access to the tasks for which aging qualifies them. Young people may come to suspect that frenzied parental lives are not the model they should emulate. The popular song of a decade ago, "Stop the World, I want to get off," did not address this issue directly but it represents a sentiment felt by some youth. Certainly it is the desire of many elders who would like to get on to their appropriate agenda. It is not reality from which some youth and many elders would escape; it is that limited aspect of the life cycle which adults try to equate with reality.

Happily for the process of aging, increasing numbers of men and women are acknowledging mid-life dissatisfactions with middle-class adulthood. Over the past decade there has been growing evidence of the unrewarding style of life calculated to assure success. Gail Sheehy's *Passages* is but the most recent and most widely read of such books. Both her timing and the manner of her approach make it possible for increasing numbers of people to acknowledge restlessness with prevailing middle-class burdens. Such vexations as commuting, car-pooling children, cocktail parties which don't refresh, are obvious. More important are the covert burdens arising from the concealments in which most of us are involved. Let me quote again the observation of one of the wisest of contemporary therapists.

> . . . most people do not admit to themselves feelings of fear, boredom, loneliness, hopelessness—that is to say, they are unconscious of these feelings. This is so for a simple reason. Our social pattern is such that the successful man is not supposed to be afraid or bored or lonely. He must find this world the best of all worlds; in order to have the best chance for promotion he must repress fear as well as doubt, depression, boredom, or hopelessness.[3]

This is an inhuman burden, but is it any less inhuman to deny older people the opportunity to unburden themselves of such deceptions and to get on to their appropriate tasks? That the wisdom of age is so helpful to all of us only adds to the irony of our refusal to allow people to grow older.

Two matters have emerged from recent reflection which I want to share in praise of aging. That they are paradoxical may be just what adults need to learn about life. The first is that strength is strongest which least conceals its weaknesses. The second is that faith is more influential which acknowledges its doubts. Likewise, the inward movement characteristic of aging is complemented by a new affection for things and people outside oneself. This is the double thrust of aging. It is also my contention that the latter flows from the success of the former. Inadequate self-acquaintance leaves one, of whatever age, able to view the world only in terms of how much can be gotten out of it for oneself. As George MacDonald said of his adolescent hero, he had come ". . . to believe in nothing but his dinner: to be sure of a thing . . . is to have it between his teeth."[4]

The simplest way to consider the elders' internal journey is to remember the fact that just because we can conceal feelings from ourselves does not mean that we haven't had them or that they vanish. Because they lie beyond our control feelings simply happen; we are able either to acknowledge them and act accordingly or to let them find some inappropriate mode of expression. In the latter case the person is out of touch with aspects of his/her own life story.

Detachment from our own story is clearly possible and in some ways desirable. To be constantly in touch with the necessarily limited resources of our own origins would be a handicap. We are a fluid society and, as the child of immigrant parents, I would not have it otherwise. But there is a price for such detachment. While we may be willing to pay it for many years, it is perilous to continue to do so indefinitely. As Erikson indicates in his all-too-brief discussion, the achievement of Ego Integrity involves acceptance of the fact that one's mother and father were one's actual parents. This may seem like such an unassailable fact that mentioning it is ludicrous. But, it is more one's feelings about the fact than the fact itself with which Erikson would put us in contact. Acquaintance with one's own story means, in part, to be free from the wish that one's parents had been different. It is not the facts of our lives which make us human; it is our acknowledged relationship to those facts which may do so.

Let me illustrate how reacquaintance with one's story may illumine otherwise dark areas of one's life. Long familiar with the biblical characterization of marriage as a man and woman becoming "one flesh," it occurred to me that this union did not occur in the reasonable happy lives of my parents. My father's passiveness and my mother's aggressiveness only became "one flesh" in me. It is I who must learn to honor them by achieving an integrity which no longer wishes they might have been other than they were. Not absolutely determined by them I will be free to honor them, and be somewhat free from them, only as I acknowledge the extent to which they contributed to the concerns and style of my adult life. For as long as I wished they had been other than they were, which I take to be a fairly common attitude, I was hopelessly trapped in my refusal to embrace the significant people of my own story. Once able to acknowledge the facts of my parentage I both appreciated them anew and was somewhat freed from my self-made bondage. In order that my life may indeed be mine and not just theirs I must own their influence and be fully responsible for who I am. This is crucial work from which the business (busyness) of adulthood mustn't keep me.

Attention to their own story is partly forced upon elders by circumstances. The maturing of children, the mobility of acquaintances, the aging and death of friends does isolate the aging. However successfully one may have avoided thoughts about one's mortality (what some call "unproductive or morbid brooding"), changes in one's own body make such important knowledge difficult to avoid. Matters as simple as graying hair and slower recuperation begin to suggest a new, or at least long neglected, agenda.

One further illustration may complete this brief sketch of the first of two developments appropriate to aging. Increased attention to one's own inner life carries with it an appreciation for others' inner lives. Perhaps this is part of the reason for the child/grandparent affinity we've mentioned. In any event, after years of trying to make another over into some more acceptable image it may become clear that the other simply is what he or she is. Fatigue may contribute to this acceptance but I think that it involves something much more positive than resignation. It is a feeling of kinship with other people with whom one has shared times and places. A contemporary writer puts it succinctly:

> I have been wondering this summer why our [marital] love has seemed deeper, tenderer than ever before. It's taken us twenty-five years, almost, but perhaps at last we are willing to let each other be, as we are . . . learning not to chafe at the other's particular isness. . . .[5]

This ability to let each other be is not an easy achievement. As I reflect on it I am struck by the strange dynamics of relationships with spouse and children. How often we try to remake our spouse in our own image while we are trying to assure that our children will not be like us! At the very least we want them to avoid many of our mistakes. It is ironic that while our efforts at remaking the partner are doomed to fail, the children become ever more the children of their particular parents!

It requires an appreciation of each one's distinctive story to encompass these developments. For the very reason that children must come to terms with their parentage, must make of their diverse inheritance an integral legacy, so one's spouse must do the same. Since my wife is the child of other parents it is impossible for her to become like me. Children's independence of their parents comes only though an acquaintance with their own parental story. As they become able to recognize parents as one flesh, they are able to relate to them and to change themselves within the context of freedom. Something similar occurs in one's spouse: to undertake any voluntary re-making, which is the antithesis of being remade, s/he must be familar with his/her own story. Then, and only then, is something that might be called love possible. In the inner development intrinsic to aging lies the potential for mutual interest in others' stories. This is the grace we see in the lives of beautiful old couples.

Aging is a time when it may be possible to recover the life we have lost in living. Or, as Eliot put it elsewhere, the inward journey involves the return to our place of origin in order to "know it for the first time." This process, which the demands of adult life often make difficult, is one of the privileges of aging. It is never too late to begin to know oneself for the first time. The extent of the earlier refusal to honor one's story will determine how long it will take to recover the life lost in living. And to the extent that social pressures effectively discourage such self-acquaintance we will both be cut off from our own truth and unable to provide what others may seek from us.

It would be misleading were I to leave the impression that there are but two ways of responding to aging. There are many creative ways in which older people cope: from attention to such basics as diet and exercise to the Gray Panthers' involvement in public issues. There probably is no single prescription which can be applied uniformly. Circumstances vary not only from person to person but within the individual lives. For example, I am alternately amused and irritated by a cartoon in which one elder comments to another: "As the days dwindle down to a precious few . . . I say to hell with everybody!"[6]

What I wish to identify are two somewhat distinctive developments of which elders become capable. Not only are these not confined to older people, though the ability to nurture them may in our society be practically age-specific, they are developments needed earlier in life. In earlier years these developments will be in active tension with the appropriate preoccupation with external responsibilities. This tension persists in aging but the externality of "adulthood" is gradually replaced by the now appropriate internality. I suggest that it is by this transition that a new and potentially enlarged way of relating to the external world becomes possible. This is the elder's second normative developmental task.

Since our inception the external world has been indispensable to our well-being. Even the philosopher's ability to imagine a disembodied realm of pure forms presupposes at least some awareness of the body of the thinker! Until our bodies die we are ambiguously but firmly related to external reality. It is understanding that relationship which is difficult.

In order to bring this discussion to a conclusion let me oversimplify the complex relationship between ourselves and the outside world. We must assert ourselves in order to take from nature what we need for survival. Since there is both real and imagined uncertainty about food and shelter we invest increasing effort to minimize the uncertainties. This is true historically and is repeated in individual lives. As a society and as individual people we know that full barns, or bank accounts are something of a hedge against the future. Since nature is an ambiguous friend such aspirations are understandable. That these preoccupations of adulthood both reflect and contribute to an impoverished inner life is less obvious. It is this impoverishment which the first work of aging, the movement inward, begins to correct. As one is ever more affirmative of one's own life story a new relationship with the external world emerges. An exclusive emphasis on external exploitation and inner neglect is replaced by an appreciation of the world. The inward movement transforms the outward attitude.

Appreciation. Only a word but it gives us another world. Things and people no longer exist merely to serve our needs. They do not have or lack meaning as they fit or are excluded from our frame of reference. Paradoxically, by becoming acquainted with our own story we are made free from the need to view all reality with ourselves at the center. We continue to be important but other things and people are recognized as existing in their own right. By loving acquaintance with our own story we are freed from the desperate selfishness which could only possess, devour, and deny. We are made free to enjoy, to share, to affirm. As he put so many things gracefully, Heschel deserves to be quoted at this point. "Just to be is a blessing; just to live is holy. The moment is the marvel. . . ."[7]

There is danger in these emphases on recovering one's story and the consequent change of attitude toward the world. They may be interpreted privatistically. The inwardness of the story may seem to support a purely aesthetic understanding of the new relationship to external life. That grievous error could arise from a failure to understand one's inherently social nature.

Each of us is born into a particular family. We cannot escape the importance of this fact. Equally important, however, we are born at a particular place and time. These historical circumstances are always as important as our geneology. Particular advantages or handicaps, challenges or privileges, are inescapable ingredients of one's story. Neither are we born into nor do we live our lives in a vacuum. The particular circumstances of the period into which one is born have incalculable consequences.

If we are fortunate we have realized from the beginning that we are not self-made. Others provided for our well-being in a host of ways. Not just parents who fed and clothed us but nameless persons of earlier times—those who planted the trees whose shade we enjoy; who fashioned educational programs and founded places of worship; who created language, myths, and systems of meaning by which to understand our experience. Our legacy has been vast and varied.

In the process of recalling these ingredients of our past we may realize that our lives also reach into the future. The human story continues. In recognizing the benefactions of our own story we may be instructed about opportunities to act with reference to the legacy we shall leave. Awareness of the future which the young and the unborn will inherit is part of our changed attitude toward the external world. The ways in which men and women respond to this awakening will be as varied as are individuals. In expression of their generativity some will plant trees, others become politically active for the first time, others will seek symbol systems appropriate to the time. The form of the benefaction matters little; the desire to benefit future generations is crucial. Aging is praiseworthy to the extent that, by enabling us to reconnect with our own past, it brings about a new relationship to the future world. Capable of appreciating the marvel of the moment, we also care passionately that future generations may enjoy a comparable blessing.

CHAPTER 8

Too Many Variables?

Several religious issues have been alluded to in the discussion to this point. Those who feel that the developmental tasks lie within their abilities, now that some of the opportunities and hazards have been identified, may wish to read no further. If the claims of life's stages seem humanly possible, they may simply get on with their developmental tasks.

I am among those who believe otherwise. The opportunities for growth at any life stage, which may be understood and even desired, may lie beyond one's capability. Therapy may help but growth is not just a matter of personal intent. Societal attitudes may thwart desirable maturation. Resources which transcend culture may be needed to empower people's capacity to defy the relatively good for something better. Therefore, there are two things to identify in the balance of this book: some of the important aspects of the relationship of Christian faith to the life cycle; and when and how extra-human aid might be properly forthcoming. It is never a matter of all or nothing at all, neither all faith and no effort nor the opposite. In every epoch there are more and less auspicious ways of considering the nature of Christian faith. At both conscious and unconscious levels expectations are engendered by unmet needs of every social configuration. A renewed appreciation of the importance of the stages of life, or at least some of them, appears today to be part of contemporary yearning.

Because I probably will offend some widely held current prejudices, two qualifications are necessary. First, I do not share the assumption that knowledge of something assures its enactment. While I cannot embrace St. Paul's categorical conviction that we are incapable of doing the good (Romans 7:18ff), I think that we are at least as prone to avoid as to affirm the change. For example, to be informed about all of the life stages may not mean that one is unhappy about being stuck at an early stage. Such people may know the good, and be facile in discussion of it, without effectively desiring it for themselves. There are deeper sources of resistance than mere ignorance. To be ambivalent about growth, which will be central to our discussion, is difficult in a society which is apparently enthusiastic about human development. To what extent the belief in the limitless potential for personal growth derives from decades of economic growth, or is influenced by changes in attitudes towards the Gross National Product, I do not know. What seems reasonably clear is that, irrespective of future economic patterns, the yearning for personal fulfillment is both deeply and uncritically grounded. The anomaly which must be made explicit is why anything as assumably desirable as personal fulfillment should actually be so widely resisted. Inasmuch as I will be both exhorting to growth and acknowledging the extent to which we refuse it, readers may be irritated for seemingly contradictory reasons. Given our naive confidence in the inevitability of growth I see no better alternative than to forewarn of this possibility.

Second, I shall assume that our lives are largely determined by the past. This will irritate those who believe that there are no limits to human will. I do not understand this denial of limits, but it is widely held. Many cling to the conviction that, if only they want strongly enough to do something. "I could quit if I wanted. . .!"—there are no necessary limits. Of greater sense to me is the paradox that the rebirth of the will lies in recognition of its impotence. By doing so I offend both those who believe that anything is possible and those for whom human bondage is total and irreversible. The assertion that acknowledged impotence is the route to strength will not be popular. Many would rather suffer unproductive guilt than to recognize the extent to which lives are determined. Few recognize the freeing effect of being able to get on with the limited growth which is within one's capacity. To be able to accept limits as the condition for the exercise of one's freedom, especially with reference to the claims of the life cycle, will not be easy.

The discussion will be theological but not always in a manner with which some may be familiar. It is with the claims of the life cycle, and with what may be the limitations of people's abilities to actualize life's ordinary claims, that we are concerned. It will, therefore, be with reference to these claims that our theological discussion will develop. We will be doing theology backwards: starting with some aspect of human experience to discover its relevance to the Christian tradition.

In popular usage, and for the convenience of discussion, we talk about a life stage, such as adolescence, as though it were an entity unrelated to what preceded it and what will follow. The arbitrariness is, I believe, unavoidable but it is inherently misleading. We cannot be too clear about this matter. It is one of Erikson's contributions to have seen that all of the stages are potentially present at each stage. That is, there are resources inherent at all of the stages which a mature person should be able to draw upon for dealing with an issue particular to a specific stage. For example, the adolescent struggling within initial sexual self-awareness needs to realize that the impulse to self-gratification must be balanced by a capacity for intimacy. The onset of sexual capability requires youth, often for the first time, to recognize responsibility for the future. Similarly, the older person struggling with the threats to meaning which inhere in aging needs to be able to draw upon resources for sensual enjoyment. The life stages are both distinguishable and inseparable, not to be confused with one another yet constantly influencing each other.

The solution lies in recognizing the fact of configurations. Neither the life cycle nor Christian doctrine is a series of unrelated entities. At any life stage a particular set of tasks determines the configuration of one's total resources. For example, those in the process of proving themselves capable of intimacy have less need of their capacity for solitude than may be required at another time. Becoming capable of intimate relationships determines, at that stage, the particularly appropriate configuration. Relevant resources come, hopefully, to hand; those less relevant to that task are, for the time, marginal. Similarly, to focus upon one doctrinal affirmation means that the other ingredients will be arranged in a configuration determined by their relevance to the item one is seeking to understand.

This dynamic understanding of the similar character of both the cycle of life and of Christian faith indicates why clarifications will be neither easy nor to everyone's satisfaction. Not only are we working with two sets of variables, but with the integral relationship between them. This will involve us in a double arbitrariness and will compound the potential for being misleading. We will, for example, stop the camera as though it were possible to view one of life's frames. While looking at such a still we shall suggest one or more aspects of doctrine which may be relevant to the life-task so stopped. The possibilities for illumination of issues both in personal maturation and in Christian doctrine are considerable; the dangers are no less real.

Theologians may well be displeased with the distortions which result from my preoccupation with the claims of the life cycle; social scientists may object to the assertion that life cycle claims drive one beyond ordinary human resources. It would be more convenient not to try to suggest their mutual inter-relationship. To refuse the task would, however, contribute to both the despair which is latent in the life cycle and to the suspicion that Christian faith is relevant only within its own, self-defined, sphere. Since I am both involved in the stages of life and am a Christian believer, I choose to run the risks of bringing together two understandings of human experience. It is not my intent to produce another psychology of religion nor to argue for the sole sufficiency of faith. Rather, respecting both traditions in which I am personally involved, I hope to suggest the excitement and the relevance of a Christianity which recognizes that the tasks presented by the stages of human life are gifts from God.

This recognition rests on two basic convictions. First, I believe that progress through the stages of the life cycle is important not only for understanding the work of human maturation but for growth in faith. The material to which faith must respond arises in large part from the tasks of each life-stage. Second, it is central to faith's work to encourage us, especially when fear inhibits, to engage the risky steps in our growth to maturity. Thus, growth and faith are correlative. The imperatives to personal growth endlessly generate challenges to further maturation. And Christian faith both affirms these developmental tasks as from God and empowers us to embrace life's questions when, as is often the case, we'd rather not. It is central to my argument that we recognize in the seasons of our lives the ordinary means by which God seeks to bring us to faith rather than to despair.

Some will recognize that there is at least tension, perhaps even an impasse, between a traditional understanding of Christian theology and my emphasis on personal growth. There seems to be a conflict between the givenness of the faith—Scripture and the church's history—and the dynamic struggle for growth. At least part of the solution lies in recognizing that our perceptions of the unchanging do, in fact, change. With this recognition God's continuity is preserved while we acknowledge the processes through which we pass in the stages of life. To be empowered by God is to be in the process of change! It is, I believe, one of the distortions of Christianity to view faith as an ally in one's personal effort to resist change. The tension between continuity and change is inherent in human experience.

I suspect that the roots of our ambivalence to change lie at a deep level. It may be difficult enough to encompass the knowledge explosion and the computerization of much of life but these are superficial difficulties compared with the demand for self-knowledge. Whereas they require us to revise our way of thinking, which itself is never easy, self-knowledge calls for a new way of being. Whether or not it lies within our power to do this will be a recurring issue. But, we must first admit that personal change is something we both want and avoid. A wise old woman put the difficulty clearly: ". . .'Know thyself' is still the unbearable command. . . . It does take the heart of a hero to even glance at what one hopes is the wavering line of growth."[1] At age eighty-two, this Jungian analyst suggested that it is by the hard work of affirming all that has been true about our lives that we become "fierce with reality." Probably most people desire to be more intensely alive, more vivid. I suspect also that this is the growth which most of us find too costly. At one level we would like to be different, at another we fear it. We want growth's gain but we grieve the anticipated loss.

Part of the problem is that we don't know what to do with the parts of our lives which have been unattractive or actively harmful. Unable to hope, to embrace both good and bad sides, some people are confined to lives of concealment. So energetic are we in this that we may even hide from ourselves the realities of our own lives. Is it surprising that we are often fatigued? Is it surprising that we are simultaneously intrigued and irritated to meet someone who is more in touch with him/herself? To be so "fierce with reality" is, I believe, God's desire for us all. Perhaps it is only by Another so fiercely real that we will be helped to move beyond our ambivalence to change, to embrace growth as our vocation from God.

It is with the traditional center of faith that I am concerned; it is with the holy in our midst. Somewhat untraditional is the context within which we seek the presence of grace. It is my incarnationally derived conviction that it is in the stages of our lives, and especially at those times of transition from one stage to the next, that the search for ultimate meaning is both most promising and most perilous. Whatever else sin may be, it is certainly present in the refusal to locate the holy and to respond to grace at critical points in the life-cycle.

We are dealing with a conflict between two bases for understanding human nature. At one extreme are those who look to nature for guidance; at the other are those who insist that history alone produces what is distinctively human. Even as I write these sentences I realize how imprecise are such terms as "human nature," "nature," and "history." Each involves millennia of ponderings, definitions, arguments, even warfare. At issue are at least two questions: 1) What sorts of experiences are necessary for the making of human lives? 2) What are the barriers which most effectively discourage people's realization of their humanity? Recognizing that clarification of the questions may be all that's possible in a few pages, let's consider each briefly.

The question of necessary experiences might be seen as a disagreement between those who insist on the inevitability of conflict and those who believe that human development is essentially non-conflictual. The former are the proponents of history-as-determinative; the latter see nature as the shaper of lives. The former stress the importance of decision-making, of responsible choices; the latter call for recognition of and alignment with the natural flow of lives. The former assume resources of will and defiance; the latter the emergence of wisdom and of acceptance. Perhaps no single person occupies either of these positions as described; probably all find themselves primarily drawn to one but find neither able to account for all relevant facts. Neither history nor nature can be ignored if we are to understand what it might be to be human. The task is to discover ways by which both may be affirmed without the reduction of either. I believe that the developmental model provides a basis for such affirmation.

While the model assumes physiological and societal prompt-ings toward the development of maturity, neither of these is determinative. Things may happen in our bodies—things as dissimilar as the onset of puberty and of senility—without requiring any necessary maturation of the person. For some adolescents puberty is the occasion for regression rather than growth. As mentioned before, Hannah Greene's novel, *I Never Promised You a Rose Garden*, emphasizes the price paid by those able to make only tentative steps towards a viable adulthood. Nor is evidence lacking to remind us that, at least in this society, chronological aging often prompts desperate efforts to recover, or at least to try to conceal the loss of, one's youth. The possibility that people will not be prompted towards maturity simply by biological change is just as strong as the possibility that they will.

Nor is social pressure more able than is biology to assure growth. Institutions may be created to accomplish certain developments. These may be even generally effective for shaping many people's behavior. Except for the simplest of tasks, however, it is impossible to determine uniform results. At least two facts seem to militate against the social determinism of Orwell's nightmare, *1984*: the difficulty of programming complex results and the ambivalences within each human life. Perhaps one illustration will suffice. It is impossible so to organize social institutions to produce only a certain kind of adult male or female because several things are unattainable. These are: societal agreement as to the desired goal; programming to assure only one result; and, in many individuals, the inability to settle for only that which has been included in any model. For example, every man and woman needs to be capable of both toughness and tenderness; all are both dependent and independent in different circumstances. Even were societal agreement about a single goal and programming capability possible, a human person has and needs contradictory capabilities. Several decades ago Karen Horney wrote an important book about the contradictions in American attitudes which resulted in a distinctive form of neurosis. In *The Neurotic Personality of Our Time* she identified our ambivalence about the importance of cooperation and competitiveness as the cause of the maladies which brought patients to her. In our present society the dilemma is unresolvable. We have the capacity and need for both cooperation and competitiveness. We seek a world view which enables us to be either depending on the situation.

Without denying the importance of both biology and sociology, should we not take into account both the fact of choosing and of the partially determined character of our choices? We cannot ignore the fact that personal decisions are being made from the center of one's being or that the content at that center is always historically-determined. On the one hand, whether I acknowledge it or not, I am always the person who determines my relationship to the biologically and sociologically derived agenda at any given moment. It is the fact that I choose which makes me an historical being. On the other hand, the range of possibilities from which I may choose is always determined by both my time and place and my personal history of decision-making or decision-avoidance. To be a person is to be embodied, to belong to a social body, to live at a particular time and location, to have acted in certain ways. And yet, despite these determining factors, to be a person means that the next act cannot be utterly predictable. Are not these the components which go into the making of a human life? What, then, makes the process of humanization so difficult?

All of the material of comedy and tragedy is here. So, with one exception, is the material of theology. The only matter lacking is our attitude towards this complex mix of determining factors and personal accountability. Am I but the unwitting consequence of forces over which I have no control? Or, admitting the reality of these forces, is there some sustaining sense in which I can affirm, without destructive guilt or misinformed pride, responsibility for my life?

Let me put it as simply as possible: while the fact of the passage of time does not assure one's maturation, and while there may be exceptional experiences which are capable of accelerating growth at any point in a person's life, human lives ordinarily mature in connection with the passage of time. People are not necessarily mature because they are aged but it is one's continuous passage through ordinary experiences which is the God-given means for human development. The decisive matter for maturation is one's attitude towards these ordinary experiences. How one related to the onset of puberty or of aging determines the extent to which such experiences may be occasions for growth and for growth in faith. There may be other barriers to the realization of one's humanity but the chief obstacles take the form of two mistaken assumptions and one inability. The faulty assumptions are that personal growth simply happens with the passage of time or that the potential for growth stops at some fairly early point and one remains thereafter in a holding pattern. Those who assume that one simply grows like Topsy cannot have paid much attention to either their own experience or to the evidence from both literature and the clinician's office. The assumption that growth is natural and inevitable is usually accompanied by the failure to recognize that every developmental gain involves loss. Also obscured is the fact that loss involves grief, the acknowledgement that one has let go of some aspect of oneself previously valued and useful. The person who marries, for example, thereby demonstrating some capacity for intimacy, has given up much that went with being single. The gain may be genuinely valued but the loss is no less real. As a society we have much to learn about the reality of these losses.

Also undermining the work of human development is the assumption that the potential for growth stops at some point in one's chronological aging. Often this seems to be associated with physical maturation. It is difficult to understand what else sustains such an assumption. Perhaps the best corrective for such an attitude is the statement made by Maggie Kuhn at age seventy-five: "I've grown more in the last decade than I did in my first sixty-five years."

The inability, which is related to both of the faulty assumptions, is found in those who cannot see the continuing opportunity to growth as coming from God. For such people religious faith is, as it is often accused, regressive. Their practice of religion does not involve the regular return to the basic issues of trust and mistrust for the sake of recovering lost parts of themselves and of grappling more adequately with current developmental tasks. Rather, their sense of religion helps them to avoid the risky effort to reform either past or present. By contrast, I believe the endless willingness to take such risks, to be engaged in life-long reformation, is the mark of the life of faith.

The ordinary barriers to human development are attitudinal, which results in an avoidance of those exciting (and often frightening) experiences necessary for the making of fully human lives. That religion should ever be, or be thought of as, an ally of such growth-avoidance is as tragic as it is widespread. I suggest, rather, that the potential for growth inheres endlessly in life's stages and that this is God's ordinary means for calling us to faith by calling us to be more fully ourselves. As the experience of a widower indicates, it is relatively easy to get stuck far short of one's development potential. During a long marriage his needs had been largely anticipated by his alert wife. His loneliness and self-pity after her death were partly the result of the loss of these services. At age eighty he is learning that he must and can take some social initiative. As he becomes unstuck the loneliness is yielding! The potential for growth endures.

No single means will cause everybody to come to life. Some will be moved by a failure to be promoted; others only by the inability to enjoy, or execute, the responsibilities of a long-desired promotion. Years ago George Buttrick talked about "the ploughshare of God's sorrow." For some that will call them from a living death; others, however, will be further crushed by such experience. No prescription covers all. As indicated earlier, I was surprised by the means which prompted me to begin to pay attention to what I eventually recognized as my stalled life. I was on holiday in Norway and went to see the Vigeland sculpture. Something in his figures intrigued me. It proved eventually to be a means by which I began to reflect on my experiences of adulthood. The key to that heartening experience was that I began to realize the possibility of a new kind of growth. Largely gone was the emphasis on externals, on getting qualified and on demonstrating proficiency. These matters were well enough settled for the present. Through the sculpture, however, I came to see the potential for inner growth which far exceeded anything I then realized. There was, for example, the self which I had for so long neglected because of a variety of external obligations. Could I reestablish relationship with myself? There was the love-relationship which I had once so eagerly affirmed. Could some new bases be discovered whereby we could become again, with children grown, the mutually desirable persons we had once been to each other? There was the work to which I had perhaps too generously given myself. Could I learn with integrity and satisfaction to set limits to its demands in a work-compulsive environment? It would be misleading to suggest quick success in any of these areas. The first task, which took years to accomplish, was to recognize this largely internal agenda as mine. Only with this recognition was I able to get on with the work of self-acquaintance; of renewing the primary, voluntary relationships of my life; and of being more the master of rather than mastered by my work. It was less a matter of seeking new experiences, though these occurred, than of reworking attitudes towards myself and others in light of the changed circumstances of mid-life.

Out of these inner and relational dimensions of my life, or in tandem with them, came a new attitude towards the world. Rather than something merely to be used, the world of nature and of other people became a cause for enjoyment, for appreciation, for wonder, something I wanted to be sure that those who came after me would be able to know and value. I recently had a conversation with our son which I could not have anticipated as I walked away from the sculpture park. We were talking about gardening with which I was earlier largely unacquainted. One of the things which I learned from him is that, short of poisoning the earth, it is impossible to rid soil of its seeds. Each spring when I dig the garden in preparation for planting, an activity necessary to create an environment hospitable to whatever one wants to grow, I also create the conditions in which dormant seeds may flourish. That they are usually weeds that volunteer is not the point. They emerge because they have been given access by the digging to warmth and moisture required for their activation. It was instructive to learn that seeds in the desert may remain dormant for a century or longer until proper conditions obtain.

The analogy of this for lives is, I hope, apparent. Within each of us lies unactivated potential. For a variety of reasons the conditions for its arousal have been lacking. The soil may have become too compacted or been insufficiently watered.That some aspects of our neglected selves may be undesirable must not cause us to assume that all is weeds. If we genuinely affirm the God-givenness of our lives that couldn't be true. Now and to the very end there are latent capabilities for being ever more open to the needs and opportunities of our time and place. These will range from the widower's discovery that he was able to invite a friend to lunch to the teacher's realization that there is deeper satisfaction in encouraging students' confidence in their own abilities than there is in impressing them with one's learning. Both of these generative responses to quite different situations illustrate the variety of ways in which more constructive behavior may result from activating the neglected seed of one's inner life.

I gradually became aware of many aspects of life which I hope our society will learn to value and to help people appreciate. They may all be included under the need to pay attention. I recognized this again recently while watching The Belle of Amherst. From what limited stimulation there was in her 19th century, small-town home Emily Dickinson was able to nourish herself, and nourish us a century later. Not very much was happening but she paid loving attention to whatever did occur. As we are rarely able to be, in part because of the overload of external experience, she was attentive.

By contrast, our lives—perhaps especially in the decades from twenty to forty—are filled with diverse experiences. And we make so little of them. So busy are we that there isn't time to pay attention. And the fatigue we feel is the result both of the pace and of the fact that our inattentiveness provides little nourishment. For life to begin at forty we must learn to take time for self-acquaintance, to see and to be with others, to recognize injustice and the ways in which we contribute to it, to learn to set responsible limits to the claims of one's work, to listen to and observe what we normally don't hear or notice in the world of nature. That one cannot really see birds while moving was an important instruction. Having unsettled the occupants of an area by walking into it, you must be still and allow the creatures to become accustomed to your presence. Then, if patient, the bird-watcher will sometimes be rewarded. Having long assumed that busyness justifies lives, it is not easy to learn that new life is partly based upon the opposite assumption.

Was not this the point of Thornton Wilder's play, *Our Town?* In the last act there is a poignant plea. Returned from the Grover's Corners cemetery for one day, her 12th birthday, Emily noticed the many missed opportunities for friendship, for caring, even in intimate family life. In the slower pace of life in a New Hampshire village at the turn of the century she is struck by the extent to which busyness and habit keep people from noticing so much that's important. Before returning to her grave she cries out, "Oh Mama, just look at me one minute as though you really saw me." That her mother could not hear this call from the grave suggests how trapped we are in deadening routines. Is there reason to believe there will be widespread ability to hear the call to new life from One raised from the dead?

Life may begin at forty, or whenever one experiences the onset of mid-life. Central to such a realization, however, is the recognition that the new life is not just more of the same. It will not be a re-run of one's prior years. It will not be more frenzied accumulation of experience. God continues to call us to pilgrimage by calling us to become ever more attentive to and intentional about ourselves and our involvements wherever we may be in the life cycle. It is one of faith's gifts to enable us to affirm this invitation to the pain and reward of endless growth.

In our discussion to this point we have used the experiences of mid-life as a clue to the tensions which are inherent in the life cycle. In the final chapter we shall suggest a relationship of the Christian faith to some of these general characteristics of the life cycle. In addition to identifying these, we shall be searching for some of the important sources of resistance to human development. Why do we both desire and resist something as inherently desirable as our maturation as men and women? We shall find theology both supportive of the impetus to human fulfillment and critical of those factors within lives (personal sin) and within society (corporate sin) which distort and discourage the growth to which God calls all people. Theology will thus be both ally and enemy of people's efforts to fashion their lives. It both supports the desire to acknowledge the God-givenness of lives and resists every attempt to find security in something short of our complex wholeness.

CHAPTER 9

Beyond the Life Cycle?

It is my contention that the work of the life stages is God's ordinary means for human maturation. Consequently, it is with both the claims of each of the stages and the need to integrate past experience into present life that Christian faith must deal. Faith is not insulation against the hard choices which arise inevitably over the course of life. Rather, it is a means by which to embrace the risks and rewards of being intentional about one's actual life. To be insulated against these challenges is evidence of bad faith. Lacking trust in God one is unable to trust those potentials for development which arise from a combination of internal promptings and external expectations.

These inner and outer sources of maturation are grounded in biological and social factors. From both internal changes, over which we have no control, and social expectations, which are never as sound as societies pretend they are, human maturation may occur. Whether or not such maturity takes place depends on how well one is able to assent discriminatingly to biological inevitabilities and to societal promptings. Whether or not any particular description of the stages of human growth is to be preferred over all others, and whether or not there is a meaningful, universal, understanding of maturity, are moot points. In time such questions may be answerable but at the present we only have useful theories based on limited data. This troubles me less than does the tendency to use this fact to obscure the universal need to deal with the issues of our lives. Choices are being made constantly by all people which determine the extent to which they are becoming more or less intentional about their lives and the larger community. It is my contention that intentionality about one's own God-given potential for development is the means by which people begin to recognize their kinship with others. We have spoken earlier of the fear that this intentionality will give license to selfishness. I can only repeat my conviction that selfishness results from the inability to assign worth to one's own life and results in the inability to recognize the worth of others' lives. Whether or not one is in the process of becoming more a part of that larger life is the issue with which Christian faith is centrally concerned. If that faith is not relevant to the basic questions of one's life, then it insulates one from both self-acquaintance and awareness of the human community to which all belong. Lives informed primarily by fear refuse the invitation to maturity and will use every resource to justify the refusal. Religion is often so misused.

The combination of such misuse and of an otherworldly spirituality largely obscures the fact that faith in God leads to ever deeper awareness of the realities of one's own life and a consequent concern for the lives of others. The way to healthy relationships with others, within which I include the possibility of personal sacrifice, is by intentionality about one's own life. (Exhortations to self-sacrifice are trivialized to the extent that the worth of the self is denied. No pain is involved when that which is to be sacrificed is of little value. Self-sacrifice is the ultimate demand only when the God-given worth of the self is affirmed.) I am convinced that the key to a caring, constructive relationship to others is caring attention to oneself. Careful attention to the difficult issues of one's own maturation is the source of appreciation for the hopes and trials, the strengths and weaknesses, of others. We are never better prepared to befriend the stranger than when we have already befriended kindred strangers within ourselves. Instead of paternalistic concern for others, which intends to shape others in the doer's model, I am urging an ethic which recognizes the needs and resources of others because it has first recognized them in oneself. Thus do I understand Jesus' conjoining of love for neighbor and for self.

I am increasingly impatient with two attitudes: that intentionality about one's life is natural, needing no faith-grounding to sustain it; and, at the other extreme, that such intentionality will foster selfishness. To those who hold the former I must say that the evidence is unconvincing. The risks inherent in progress through the conflicting claims of the life stages are always as intimidating as exhilarating. Most people find ways either to avoid or to diminish those claims. A life needs to be adequately grounded in order to be able to affirm the ambivalences of each of the life stages. Any approach to life which abhors contradiction will be forced to suppress one side of any ambivalence. Pretense or resignation then become the substitutes for faith-informed affirmation. Concealment of one's inability to affirm life's ambivalences has destructive consequences both for that person and for those with whom s/he deals. The tragedy of the over-burdened pretender is at least matched by the suffering of the one driven to resignation.

The Christian task is to be able to embrace the ambivalences of every life stage because they are unavoidable. Every need for pretense is dysfunctional. Every desire for less pretense, which is always risky and may be threatening to others, needs to be grounded in the double confidence that greater truthfulness of self-presentation lies within one's capability and that, in the long run if not immediately, it will benefit others. The source of such confidence is the believer's awareness of the divine initiative encountered in the human struggles of Jesus as the Messiah. The willingness to engage the seemingly incompatible polarities of each life stage is thus not a matter of natural inclination. Naturally, one avoids risk unless there is reason for taking it. For the Christian that reason is the desire to love God with one's whole being. Both pretense and resignation, however pious their appearance, fail to love because they have refused the risks of comprehensive self-acquaintance.

The charge that intentionality about one's life inevitably leads to narcissism does seem possible. But it is unlikely. While one's own life is endlessly interesting to that person, the roots of narcissism are not to be located in paying proper attention to oneself. Quite the opposite is the case. Narcissism, and the selfishness it engenders, is the consequence of inattention to the tasks of the life stages through which one passes. Not having wrestled successfully with these tasks such persons are handicapped in two important ways. First, they lack appreciation of their actual strengths and weaknesses, and therefore are trapped in narcissistic fantasies about their own power, beauty, or intelligence. Second, ignorant of their actual but imperfect viability they are unable to reach out to and be nourished by the external world. In this inability we encounter one of the paradoxes of human life, that we must love ourselves in order to love others. That this, which Jesus himself used as the second part of his succinct summary of Jewish Law, has been played down by Christians has been the source of much harm. This negative attitude has discouraged attention to the issues of one's own inner development. For reasons which thoughtful observers of life have long noted, hatred follows directly upon fear. I assume that unfamiliarity with oneself easily leads to selective self-loathing. We are able to approve only the better aspects of ourselves. Such ignorance of self blinds us to our similarities with others. First we fear the alien, but soon we hate. Unwilling to give anything to others, we are equally unable to receive. This is clearly seen with reference to the unacceptable aspects of one's own life. Anything about ourselves with which we have not come to terms such as the fact of growing older will appear doubly repugnant when seen in others. The irony of such unfamiliarity with ourselves is that it shuts us off from the nourishing comradeship we might have enjoyed with others similarly afflicted.

It is, I believe, by attention to one's self and by engaging the struggles inherent in personal growth that one is able to relate accurately and caringly to the larger world. The capacity for self-denial is the fruit of a proper self-love. The duty to deny one's self on the assumption that one's life is worthless only assures the very selfishness which the framers of the original obligation sought to avoid. Such exhortations obscure the fact that, in Christ, God has confirmed the high valuation of human lives which is reported throughout Hebrew Scriptures. This confirmation is not the source of glib satisfaction with the status quo. Rather, God's confirmation of one's inherent worth is the assurance which motivates to persistent intentionality about the progress of all lives toward maturity. The need is not for techniques which enable us to conceal our impairments. Rather, acknowledgment of one's limitations is the basis for relationships between imperfect persons. Deception destroys the basis for mutuality.

Two further clarifications remain to be made. First, in language somewhat different from that used by writers on human development, we must recognize the constant presence of pairs of variables which influence the ways in which different individuals respond to the challenges of the stages of life. (Actually the urgency of these polarities varies from season to season within every particular life.) Second, we must address the fundamental difference between the assumptions which inform the social sciences and those by which the arts are shaped. In the conflict between the former's quantified generalizations about lives and the latter's insistence on the qualitative uniqueness of each life we will see a central task for theology. While every individual life deviates somewhat from the normative prescriptions of social science, the social sciences are not thereby invalidated. While all persons have infinitely more in common than is unique to any life, it is the combination of the shared and the unshared which must be affirmed. It is in the potentially creative tension between all that we share with all others and our own distinctive way of responding to the world that mature humanity is found. It is a central function of Christian faith to enable believers to maintain that tension. Every temptation to absolutize either human likeness or individual uniqueness must be resisted. That is why theology is both necessary and awkward. Derived from an understanding of the divine initiative which reaches out to humankind as a whole and to individuals in particular, Christian theology requires affirmation of universal kinship and personal distinctiveness. Herein is the burden and glory of God-given and God-confirmed humanity: to be neither reducible to nor fully removable from humankind.

It is Christ's kinship with all persons which endlessly nurtures hope for the maturation of ordinary lives in the direction of his humanity. Just what the original disciples' experience of Christ risen may have been remains inexplicable.

The reports in the New Testament are attempts to point to a decisive, hope-engendering experience which was associated inseparably with the executed Jesus. That the event was historically unique explains why no report of it will ever be adequate. Historical descriptions presuppose similarities of events with each other but this event was one-of-a-kind. With reference to all other happenings of human history, this was the non-happening by which the believer is able to make some sense of all the others. It is in relationship to this non-event that the believer begins to see the possibility of new life based on affirmations of the resurrection of the body and everlasting life. Careful exploration of either of these expressions would require more skill and space than is at our disposal. For present purposes, however, we may say that the fact of Christ's resurrection has a bearing upon human bondage to societally-determined selfhood or to a sense of self which rejects kinship with others. Both bondages are forms of death not easily escaped. To be rescued requires drastic means. Finding oneself so rescued the believer experiences hope for the rebirth of the body and self, and hope for an everlasting life. The energies formerly dissipated in either of these bondages are freed for affirming the ambivalences of social determinism and personal initiative. To be capable of such affirmation is the new life to which the believer is raised; to engage the everlasting tasks of this new life is life everlasting. Every such engagement with the God-given truth about human life is inherently everlasting. Inasmuch as reality has therein been encountered and appropriated and the truth has been done, however incompletely, the gains for self and others endure. In the face of apparent evidence to the contrary this may be the most difficult assurance to sustain. Whatever else the framers of the Creed may have intended by the article on everlasting life, this assurance is an integral ingredient of it: life willingly lived in conformity with the truth about its inescapable tensions is its own justification and bears good fruit. To be unable to affirm this results in both cynicism about the worth of one's own life and all others. The durability of such destructive attitudes suggests both the depths at which sin is rooted and the radical means required to overcome it.

In order to get at the pairs of variables, which is one of the two issues to be dealt with in conclusion, it is necessary to recall some of the reasons why people balk at the demands of the life stages. Some of the resistance is the result of ignorance and will yield to information; other sources of resistance seem to originate in an aversion to the inescapable realities of human life. The latter is nowhere more clearly seen than in the abhorrence which many people feel for contradiction. At the extreme there are men and women who suffer profoundly and inflict much suffering on others by their inability to tolerate contradiction. In this, I believe, they yearn for a world which, because of ambivalences which are inherent in our humanity, never was nor ever will be. While we shall discuss a few of these at greater length it might be useful at this point to indicate that by constitutive ambivalences I refer to such polarities as the male and female ingredients in every human being; the endless tension between the need for initiative and acceptance of inevitability; the conflict between our similarities to all others and our distinctiveness from them; the tension between self-giving and gaining for oneself; the inevitability of gains and losses which inhere in every experience. The Serenity Prayer of Alcoholics Anonymous well captures the nuances of all the polarities with which we must learn to deal: "God, give us grace to accept with serenity the things that cannot be changed, courage to change the things that should be changed, and the wisdom to distinguish the one from the other."

Such constitutive realities are inherently inseparable. Creativity and wholeness reside in the capacity to hold together elements which tend to fly apart. Deep in the human makeup, however, is the desire to destroy the indestructible tension which I believe to be God-given. Some effort to minimize the tensions is undoubtedly universal and tolerable, but successful destruction of them is perilous. The fact of contradiction must not be understood as sin or the consequence of it. To the contrary, sin seeks to destroy the potentially creative tensions inherent in such universal human polarities as our complex sexuality, our capacities for both action and passivity, our likeness to others and our uniqueness. The appeal of this desire, with which all are familiar, is the false promise that it is possible to escape the complex burden of human freedom. This effort to achieve simplification by ignoring aspects of reality leads to the distortions of machismo, of compulsive aggressiveness or quiescence, of attempted loss of identity in mass society or the need always to appear to be different. Such distortions undermine the basis for both mutual love and human community. The need to conceal aspects of one's actual life destroys the awareness of kinship which is basic in all such relationships.

The underlying issue is whether or not one is sufficiently aware of the divine initiative to be able to exercise personal freedom. The ability to achieve a constructive balance of life's inherent ambivalences depends upon one's capacity for choosing. Such awareness of the divine source of one's freedom creates only the possibility for this balance. The risks are endless, the errors all too frequent. But the possibility of error is no cause for abandoning freedom. In its very nature freedom includes the possibility of misuse. The point is that such freedom is the God-given means by which the ambivalences of human experience may be appropriately and temporarily resolved. That they are never resolved perfectly or permanently must be emphasized. Imperfection is the human condition. The glory of a human life lies not in its perfectability but in its willingness to grapple with and to be rewarded by the complementary polarities which inhere in all lives. It is not, for example, the age of the elderly which must be concealed; rather, it is the enduring youth of the aging which must complement their years. Both facts are true. To be unable to affirm both is to be personally deprived and to be incapable of making one's appropriate contribution to the larger society. Thus, impoverishing patterns of concealment persist and become stronger in both the person and the society when they might have been arrested.

Consider the ways in which self-assertion and self-giving vary in daily experience. The very assertiveness, for example, which seemed appropriate to one circumstance has to be replaced in the next by appropriate yielding. Having noted earlier the emptiness which underlies all compulsive selfishness, it is necessary to note on the other side that those whose work involves regular self-giving need opportunity for renewal. A healthy adulthood is characterized by its freedom to respond appropriately to the needs of varying circumstances. Part of that freedom includes the recognition, often ignored in outsiders' opinions about the helping professions, that those who give generously of themselves to others are in more than ordinary need of opportunities for self-renewal.[1]

Of the polarities which involve continuity and discontinuity the first is that of our relationship to others. We are in ways like all other people and in ways unique. My own experience supports the observation of Anne Morrow Lindbergh that age significantly influences whether one emphasizes kinship with or distinctiveness from others. To undergraduates at her *alma mater* in the year of her fiftieth reunion she said that she felt closer to people as she grew older.

> You have experienced so much, both of happiness and sorrow; you have made so many mistakes—and survived them—that you feel you can understand almost everyone you meet. When I was young I felt more solitary and special. I thought I was different from everyone else. Now I have learned how similar our experiences are under our different disguises—how alike we are under our defenses. Now I am old, I feel less isolated and more compassionate; less critical and more sympathetic. . . .[2]

The tension between the continuity of kinship and the discontinuity of difference persists but the emphasis changes over the years. At no time can we simply lose ourselves in any group but never are we as isolated as we sometimes feel.

While Anne Lindbergh did not speak in that address of the unburdening which age makes possible, it seems appropriate to take account of that here. It is almost unavoidable that youth seeks to distinguish itself from the environment of origin. Simply to be somebody's child does not take adequate account of the potentialities and aspirations of a young person. To be able to emerge from the seemingly undifferentiated milieu of one's family is an important expectation in our society. The emergence may be gradual and calm or rapid and traumatic but it must not be thwarted. To become an adult we are required to distinguish ourselves from the family and circumstances of our origin. In the process many find it necessary to think of themselves as different from everyone else. There is exhilaration in feeling special. Less noted is the burden of maintaining at all times the fact of one's uniqueness. In addition to the gradually acquired, healthy appreciation of the similarity of people's experience, I want to add (as impetus to such appreciation) the desire to abandon some of the fatiguing burdens of uniqueness which always involve considerable pretense. Pretense may not be the most serious of sins but it is surely one of the most exhausting. There is joy in being able to acknowledge that one's continuities with others are at least as real as one's differences.

It is important to emphasize that it is not biology alone on which our likeness to others is based. There are opportunities for growth which come on universally. These developmental assignments have their own timetable. While they may be handled out of phase, and are endlessly being reworked as we seek inner resources with which to respond to new circumstances, there are optimal times for coping with each task. For example, the opportunity to resolve the tension between the desire for intimacy with others and for keeping one's distance depends upon the prior achievement of a viable identity. Such a sense of one's self is the precondition for entering into those relationships in which one is able both to reveal and to receive comparable disclosures from others. To be invited to intimacy while one's identity is still more diffused than clarified may be crippling. At the least, intimacy will not be achieved: the preconditions of an identity-derived trust in self and consequent ability to trust the other are lacking. Mutual misuse is not intimacy. One of the important paradoxes of human development seems to be that the achievement of a sense of uniqueness is the means by which one becomes capable of relating to those who are different. It is awareness of discontinuity which, in part, makes possible the affirmation of continuity with others.

We share a universal developmental agenda; what we make of these opportunities varies with individuals. These are the fundamental social sources of our kinship with humankind and of our inability ever to be equatable with any other person. The circumstances of one's life—i.e., unique genetic inheritance and time and place of birth—assure that the way in which one develops will be unique. It is the similarity of our adaptations which makes community possible; it is the differences in adaptation which preclude 1984. All, for example, must come to terms with the universal fact of death; no two will do so in exactly the same way. The differences may be minimal; they will persist.

It is a commonplace that it is with the reality of evil that Christian faith is concerned. The difficulty is to recognize evil in some of its subtle disguises. Two of its forms may be recognized in the claims of life's stages. The first is straightforward: evil is at work in every refusal to affirm the forward impetus of the life cycle. Every effort to sustain the present indefinitely or to dwell in the past is to be resisted. This is not to be indifferent to either the past or the present; rather it is to insist that the dynamic of life is forward. It is characteristic of a vital Christian faith to recognize and resist every tendency to downplay the claims and promise of the future.

The second form which evil often assumes in this context is to be seen in the refusal to accept the impossibility of resolving any of life's stages perfectly. It is this aversion to imperfection, often mistakenly identified as the Christian attitude, which undermines commitment to life's forward dynamic. People unable to tolerate imperfection cannot recognize that some resolution of the tasks of a particular life stage does enable one to move on to the claims and opportunities of the next. That one may be less than perfectly ready for it is no adequate reason for refusal. Some intentional delay may be wise; we are not urging headlong advances by those clearly not equipped for the demands of any next stage. We are always called to successive tasks before we are completely ready for them. Constantly to need more time and more complete evidence evinces the presence of evil which it is faith's task to overcome. It was not that Israel was a faultless people that God took initiative on their behalf, nor that God rewarded human perfection by being present in the person of Jesus Christ. The glory of the Gospel is not the obligation to be faultless. Rather, it is that in imperfection the believer may grasp evidences of the divine presence and have a heart for the tasks at hand. They will always be imperfectly accomplished. That is the nature of lives. The point is, however, that trying and not succeeding perfectly is always to be preferred to refusing to try. Such refusal is symptomatic of the attempt to escape life. Faith's work is to encourage the believer to be responsive to the claims of the present, leaving to God whatever imperfection made the believer incapable of meeting the claims fully. In this combination of responsiveness to opportunity and tolerance for one's imperfection lies the potential both for being useful and for a genuine, if incomplete, happiness.

The second of the polarities in which we experience the endless tension between life's continuity and discontinuities is in our relationship to time. It is in this context that we shall consider briefly the polarities of determinism and change. Clearly, the dynamic of life is toward the novelty with which the future beckons, however dimly. No life is exactly the same from day to day. For even the most routine-bound person change is ongoing at least in the environment and in the body's involuntary processes. The extent to which these factors are able to influence one's outlook will vary with individual circumstance: the warmth of the early spring sunshine will be able to unfreeze only some inner lives. Few people, however, are trapped in utterly unchanging patterns of response. All, I believe, would like to be able to break out of some of the compulsive responses to familiar stimuli. Many are resigned to the power of habit to confine them. The task always is to maintain the tension between appreciation for the past and hope for the future so as to be open to the possibilities and obligations of the present. The perils arise chiefly in one of two debilitating attitudes towards the past: either submitting to it as wholly determining one's responses to events or so lacking appreciation for one's life as to believe that total change is necessary. In the former we see resignation to life's continuity; in the latter the expectation of radical discontinuity. Neither extreme takes account of enough of reality: there is always more to any life than the past explains but no life is possible which lacks all connection with it.

One of the virtues of a developmental understandng of human life is that it takes both continuity and discontinuity seriously. Nothing is clearer on the Eriksonian model than that one's ability to cope with the demands of any particular stage is significantly influenced by the accomplishments of prior stages. One brings from the past resources with which to make sense of present tasks. Thus, the adult's attitude towards children and their future well-being will be characterized as primarily caring or indifferent depending on the ways in which prior polarities were resolved. On this model the fact of continuity over the years is clearly affirmed.

And, whatever the quality of one's development, this emphasis is sound. Whoever we are, whatever our adequacies and inadequacies, we must be able to assent to our present life both for itself and in order that any change may be possible. To be able to be truthful about who we now are, and to affirm responsibility for the past by which we have been shaped, are the prerequisites to a responsible present life and to future hope. Nothing good comes from wishing that we were something other than we are. Such an attitude reflects a fundamental disrespect for oneself. That the potential may be less than one sees in others, or may actually be quite limited, misses the point. On a developmental model there is no basis for comparisons with others. Lives have varied capabilities. The one thing that matters is the direction in which one is generally headed. That it be willingly towards the future is crucial. The distance covered will never be the same for all. We are like each other only in the destination we seek and in the unevenness of our progress.

To be able to recognize the continuities of one's life is, paradoxically, one of the keys to the discontinuity of human development. Without such honesty there is no firm ground from which adaptations may be possible. And these possibilities come on inexorably with the passage of time. Resigned to the determinations of the past, each new opportunity for growth may appear as yet another occasion for self-condemnation. If we are aware of these opportunities as evidence of the divine initiative then we may be able to affirm the possibility for change. Of no life may we say that it is hopeless, that there is no lingering capacity for good. The actualization may be long in coming. That is of no consequence. There may be little to be brought forth. That, too, is inconsequential. What matters is that there is something to recover and that it is never too late for it to happen. The proportions of the discontinuity are irrelevant.

They will always be modest at first. It will not be the change of which others may be capable. It will, however, be one's own. The cost of reworking and revising long-established habits will be considerable. Willingness to pay the price will be determined both by one's recollection of the destructiveness of the old ways and by slowly emerging rewards of the new. The emerging self will not be utterly unrecognizable; many may not quickly realize that anything is different. We will not become wholly different persons. But something will be new, the old bondage of the past will have been broken. Perhaps the following words from a distinguished lady who was an arrested alcoholic for the last twenty years of her life, will be instructive at this time: "O Lord, I ain't what I wanna be. O Lord, I ain't what I oughta be. O Lord, I ain't what I'm gonna be. But thanks, Lord, I ain't what I usta be."

Our involvement in time reveals, as do all the fundamental polarities with which we must deal, the ongoing tension between continuity and discontinuity. At different periods of our lives we may feel comfortable emphasizing different things. In Christian faith and in the claims of the successive life stages it is always the potential discontinuities of the future to which we must remain open. The paradox is that this capacity for responding to novelty depends directly on appreciation for one's past and on the realization that it is past. What has been is a continuing source of gain to the extent that it enables one to cope more adequately with the demands and opportunities of the present. It is to be honored for what it was, however flawed, and for what it enables us to make of the present and to hope for in the future. Perched between memory and hope it is only in this moment that God may be God for the believer. Past and future are never ends in themselves; they are positive dimensions of a Christian life only to the extent that they enable the believer to be responsive to the divine initiative in the opportunities of the living present. Whether anything short of awareness of God's continuing initiative can enable one creatively to affirm the tension between memory and hope each person must determine.

Another of the polarities which illustrate the ongoing tension between continuity and discontinuity is the matter of gains and losses. We speak of this again because our society wants to believe that only gains are cumulative. This attitude, in which there is an important element of truth, undermines the ability to be intentional about the work of life's stages because that work unavoidably involves both gains and losses. Real and valued losses accompany every developmental gain. Even when the gain is desired and achieved we must not ignore the accompanying loss. Consider these illustrations from some of life's stages. The child venturing into the excitement of the block loses the familiarity and comparative safety of the yard. The adolescent venturing into an intellectual world in which nothing may be assuredly knowable loses the certainties of childhood. The young adult venturing into the demands and rewards of intimacy leaves behind the innocence of inexperience. Persons in mid-life questioning the worth of their work both gain a lost freedom and lose a source of self-assurance. Aging persons who gradually embrace the fact of their mortality lose a precious, if misguided, illusion. To these we might add illustrations from within a life quite apart from the transitions between stages: e.g., the person who decides to become more expressive, or to take steps to become more self-aware, or to try to see things from another's point of view. All of these may represent desirable directions in which to move. That from which one is moving away may be of less value than is the new direction. The sense of loss will not thereby be avoided. The abandonment of the familiar, however important the novelty, will never be without some grief. For what we are describing is not some external thing to which little or no feeling is attached but an aspect of one's self. It may have to go, and we may wish it, but not without regret.

To balance this emphasis on the discontinuity of loss we must recall the continuity of gains over the course of human development. In this we do not imply uninterrupted gain. Every step forward—whether out of the yard and onto the block or away from the illusion of deathlessness into the fact of one's mortality—is followed by at least the desire to return to the past. In most cases, however, despite vacillation the movement is sustained. To the gains from past experience one adds achievements in the present. In a double sense the gains are cumulative: as they are arithmetically accumulated they geometrically increase one's capacity for adding to them. That this increases one's potential for loss brings together again the tension of discontinuity/continuity.

Earlier in this section I promised to amplify my assertion about what is and is not unique to the Christian believer. Two things are to be emphasized: that, in their awareness of the divine initiative, Christians have an understanding of human life which empowers them to take developmental risks they might otherwise avoid; secondly, that the maturation to which they are called by God is no different from that of all men and women. Only two things are distinctive for the Christian: the opportunity for maturation is seen as evidence of the divine presence; and developmental failure is seen not to be the last word. The grace of the divine initiative, wherein lies the indestructible worth of each human life, is both the first and the last, life-giving word. There is an heroic quality to the Christian life and it is affirmable both in success and in failure. As the title of the chapter suggests, the relationship of Christian faith to the claims of the life stages is ultimately ambivalent. The claims of these stages are taken with greater than natural seriousness without equating progress in them with success. The stages are the ordinary opportunities for maturation but, for a host of possibly determining factors, many people's growth is arrested far short of a complete maturity. The cross remains the symbol for every Christian's life. It both empowers the believer to take risks otherwise avoided and symbolizes the limits to which every life is subject. Christianly understood, the demands of the life stages are more clearly invitation to an ever deeper involvement in life—one's own and that of others—than they are sources of condemnation. Inasmuch as they occasion guilt they may be lively means for seeking at ever deeper levels for God's renewing forgiveness. It is not falling down that matters. It is the ability to get up when one has.

We turn now to our final task: to indicate the role of theology with reference to the dissimilar attitudes of the social sciences and the arts, especially literature. Put as simply as possible it is the work of belief to enable men and women to sustain the tension between normative models of human development and the deviancy of every human life from those norms. The power of the former resides in the ability of quantitative data to present pictures of the life stages which, generally, apply to everybody. The power of art is its affirmation of idiosyncratic individual lives. The former strives for universality; the latter will not relinquish particularity. For reasons intrinsic to each they remain irreconcilable. It is not the work of theology to reconcile them; the lion and the lamb lie down together only at the end of time.

The work of Christian faith, as we have argued is twofold: to honor the partial adequacy of both of these human experiences; and, to provide motivation for maintaining the tension between the human impulses to universality and to individualism. So powerful are both of these forces, and so precarious their balance, that the theologian cannot but appear awkward and inconsistent. Depending on one's reading of any particular imbalance the theologian will have to be advocate for either the social science or the artistic concern. As circumstances modify and the balance changes s/he will lend support to that force which is threatened. But inconsistency in the cause of humanity is an accusation which some must be willing to bear. One could be accused of worse things. The problem is that consistency in either direction requires one to ignore too much of human experience. Personal existence may not be possible apart from the larger humanity into which one is born and shaped, but no person is simply reducible to the status of a community unit. That people are of the community is part of the glory of being human; that no person fits imperceptibly into that community is equally glorious.

This tension may be experienced in a variety of circumstances. For our present purposes we have tried to demonstrate it with reference to the claims of the life stages. We do not intend to take back what we have said about these stages as God's ordinary schoolhouse for the maturation of lives. The point to be stressed is that in each of the polarities the tension between the universal and the particular is experienced. Perhaps Erikson has simply identified some of the heightened instances in which persons encounter again and again the powerful, conflicting claims of the larger society and of the self. Inasmuch as he is a humanistic social scientist who knows the tension within himself it would not be surprising to discover that it was his experience which made him sensitive to data which he later saw out there. Others, with different sensibilities, might both find different data and organize it differently.

The Christian contribution lies not, I believe, in the uniqueness of its data. It may be, as some contend, that a Christian sensibility will make that observer sensitive to data to which others would pay less attention. But such a role for the believer who is a social scientist or artist is only part of what I wish to identify.

The more important role of the believer is to be spokesperson for aspects of life's fundamental tensions which are being ignored. Informed by an understanding of the divine initiative, to which the witness of both the Old and New Israel points, the believer seeks to embrace within his/her own experience (and to insist upon it in all social circumstances) the equal importance of both the universal and individual aspects of human experience. Continuity and discontinuity will endlessly be at odds. Both seek ascendancy. The tension, which I take to be the source of all creativity, is always imperiled. The burden which the believer affirms is the necessity to maintain the tension despite all efforts to destroy it. That Christ was crucified for such a witness is no surprise. That he is evidence of the divine initiative in our midst is the endless surprise.

Postscript

The understanding of Christian faith suggested here is something for which I have searched for a decade. It continues. That this search was often conducted in the wrong places is increasingly clear to me.

In earlier efforts to understand faith's function in the lives of believers I was in many ways misled by the very tradition I sought to affirm. Whereas I knew that it was not faith's central work to enable one to live according to rules, whether from Mt. Sinai or the Sermon on the Mount, I long misunderstood what was meant by the imitation of Christ. I remain convinced that Jesus *is* the believer's model. However, we need to avoid every reduction of the work of faith which merely urges duplication of his behavior. It is neither in his deeds nor in his words *per se* that the key to his importance is to be found. That key, to which his actions and his teaching point, is the way in which he resolved temptations akin to those which we encounter. Since his work began and ended with temptations, it is unlikely that these were isolated experiences. Like us, he was tempted to sin; unlike us, he refused the temptations. It is in the direction of such a life that the believer wishes to move; it is by the gracious gift of faith that such movement becomes possible.

The radical nature of this gift becomes apparent in both the challenge it brings and the resources available for responding. Both challenge and response presuppose that men and women are children of God. On this assumption, the challenge is to be perfect, to be God-like. Surprising are the resources for achieving this perfection. It is to be accomplished with one's particular abilities and limitations. People are not alike in potential but all are alike in the capacity to achieve some growth in the direction of Jesus' humanity. None are measured by the distance they cover in their lives; all are judged by the direction in which their lives move. Every exhortation which imposes identical obliga- tion on all obscures both the challenge and the diversity of humans' capabilities. There is no ground for guilt because of one's resources; there are only excuses for failing to embrace the challenge.

It is about the nature of that challenge and the consequent function of faith that greater clarity is needed. Inaccurate understanding of the challenge results in the imposition of wrong burdens on believers. The result may be either the excessive burden of an unachievable perfection or the insuffi- cient burden of expectations which some will meet with little effort. The timid, for example, can easily avoid behaviors which are prohibited. I do not believe, however, that Jesus intended either to exalt timidity or to frustrate followers with expectations incapable of realization. Neither extreme takes adequate account of both the potential and the limitations of children of God. Both extremes focus on externals which may account for the assumption that prescribed observable behavior is the evident work of faith. I wish to suggest otherwise.

The point of the imitation of Christ is not to replicate in one's life the behavior of Jesus. It is rather to see reality as he saw it in order to be able to resist the temptation to abandon one's particular God-given potential for growth. The *imitatio Christi* is both to see with his eyes, to acknowledge the challenge to be perfect, and to assent to it with such resources as one has. Not only does none of us have Jesus' abilities; nobody has quite the same gifts and limitations as anybody else. Thus, the emphasis of the imitation of Christ cannot be on universal behavioral requirements. Such would destroy many aspirants while failing adequately to challenge others. Christian work is not to become something other than one is, not to be taller or hairier or longer lived. Rather, seeing the world as God sees it and affirming the givenness of one's gifts, the work is to discover what good may be done with one's particular abilities and limitations. (Matt. 6:27)

What we must recognize for both growth in faith and progress through the life stages is that the distinctive *character* of the life tasks is more important than their *content*. Unfortunately, in both the study of human development and in the identification of the work of Christian faith, the emphasis is most often on observable content. For several reasons this is misleading: normative behavior varies from culture to culture and, within a society, from one epoch to another; and prescribed behavioral content vitiates the responsibility of men and women made free in God's image. Behavioral norms, which have continuing importance but must not be allowed to define us fully, will rarely apply perfectly in particular situations and will be both beyond and beneath the capabilities of different individuals.

I wish to assign to faith the crucial work of overcoming sin's power to conceal the nature of the work of human development. Christian behavior is not the result of applying a universal template to one's desires and understandings. Such a mechanical model both ignores the distinctiveness of lives and obscures the prior issues where the struggle of faith and sin is engaged. It is by one's basic response to these prior realities that the direction of human development is determined. These realities are the inherent ambivalences of all lives at all stages of growth. As tensions which are only relatively and temporarily resolvable, they are the normative human burden. Whether consciously acknowledged or not, how such issues are dealt with determines the content of each person's behavior.

The difficulty is that a deeply grounded life is required to be able to embrace and to sustain this burden. It is a gift of faith to recognize in ambivalence the opportunity for creative response. Since creativity involves risk many prefer the certainty of prescribed behavior. That is, many prefer slavery to freedom. The curse of all slavery is that it requires and eventually depends upon the suppression of certain truths. No free person has the right regularly to deny aspects of his/her ambivalences in order to be able to act with certainty. Such certainty ignores realities both in the self and in the situation which should inform one's decision and behavior. Thus, by abdicating one's freedom as a child of God one violates the requirement to love the neighbor as one loves one's self. It is by a willingness to risk using one's particular God-given resources that the neighbor is to be loved.

What we see perfectly with Christ's eyes is human need; what we act with are our limited capabilities. The ability to do both is faith's gift.

It is sin's work to encourage concentration on observable behavior. That sin succeeds suggests how intolerable uncertainty is. The flight from freedom is the inevitable result of the loss of faith in God and the consequent faith in one's God-given resources to respond with some appropriateness to any particular situation. That it is never within our capability to respond perfectly to any circumstance must be acknowledged. That we are always able to respond more completely to another's need than naturally we might is faith's encouragement. Such ability is the function of faith which we advance here. Where faith is lacking we find either cowardice or arrogance. Both issue from the inability to embrace life's inherent antinomies. Cowardice denies the obligation to be God-like; arrogance assumes the ability to transcend all contingency.

It is sin's work, exploiting always the deep sources of fear, to nurture single-mindedness. The emphasis, then, is on the certainty of observable behavior by which all may recognize faithfulness. Faith's work contrasts sharply with this attachment to content. Trusting the reliability of the divine initiative and respectful of one's particular and always limited resources, the person of faith both acknowledges inner ambivalences and seeks in them the sources of creative action. Faith's work is to enable the believer, against every temptation to pretend certainty, to live with the inescapable uncertainties of his/her particular life. Such self love, which issues in distinctive consideration for the neighbor, is possible only when the yearning for certainty has been replaced by trust in God whom we are to love with our whole, imperfect being.

What might the work of faith so understood mean for an understanding of the imitation of Christ? If our sense of sainthood has largely been shaped by those who sought an unachievable single-mindedness, what might its form be in a person who took as God-given the indestructible ambivalences of human experience? Our image of the saint has been formed by those who exalted an either/or approach to faith. Might that imagery be more compelling if shaped by men and women who affirmed both their certainty and their uncertainty?

What we ordinarily see as purely human experience—the movement from birth to death—is the record of God's dealings with us. It is in responding to the tasks and opportunities of these successive stages that we may become aware of the divine initiative in our midst. The maturation of lives, which is modest for all and subject to the possibility of endless reversals, is the ordinary curriculum in which we may learn of God's sustaining presence. As truant and often stupid pupils we may yet discover both the surprise of repeated new opportunities and the function of this forgiveness in God's pedagogy between the cradle and the grave. This *imitatio Christi* I affirm.

Notes

Chapter 1

1. Abraham J. Heschel, *The Prophets* (New York: Harper & Row, 1963), p. 172.

Chapter 2

1. Erik H. Erikson, "Growth and Crises of the Healthy Personality." From *Identity and the Life Cycle*, copyright © 1980 W.W. Norton and Company. Reprinted with permission of the publisher.
2. W. F. Lynch, *Images of Hope* (Baltimore, MD: Helicon Press, 1965), p. 116. Used by permission of Helicon Press, Ltd.
3. Ken Rogers, "The Crisis at Life's Mid-point." *The Saturday Review of Education*, Feb. 17, 1973. Copyright © 1973 by *Saturday Review*. All rights reserved. Reprinted with permission.
4. Nicholas Johnson, *Test Patterns for Living* (New York: Bantam Books, Inc., 1972), pp. 23 ff. Copyright © 1972. Reprinted with permission of the author.
5. See William G. Perry, *Forms of Intellectual and Moral Development in the College Years* (New York: Holt, Rinehart and Winston, 1968).
6. See Jonathan Freedman, "Happy People," *The Chapel Hill Newspaper*, February 4, 1979.
7. From "Eleven Addresses to the Lord" from *Love & Fame*

by John Berryman. Copyright © 1970 by John Berryman. Reprinted by permission of Farrar, Straus and Giroux, Inc.

8. Erich Fromm, *The Revolution of Hope* (New York: Harper and Row, 1968), p. 10.

9. Oscar Hammerstein II, "A Puzzlement," *The King and I* (New York: Random House, 1951).

10. See H.P. and P.O. Bahrick, and R.P. Wittlinger, "Those Unforgettable High-School Days," *Psychology Today*, December 1974.

Chapter 3

1. Richard Baxter, "Directions About Our Labor and Calling," *Practical Works*, vol. 1 (London: George Virtu, 1838).

2. William Shakespeare, *As You Like It*, act II, scene vii.

3. Erik H. Erikson, *Identity and the Life Cycle* (New York: International University Press, 1959), pp. 55ff.

4. Erik H. Erikson, *Childhood and Society* (New York: W. W. Norton, 1965), p. 223.

5. Erik H. Erikson, *Identity and the Life Cycle*, op. cit., pp. 97ff.

6. Allen Wheelis, *The Quest for Identity* (New York: W. W. Norton, 1958), p. 162.

7. John Calvin, "The Right Use of the Present Life and Its Supports," *The Institutes of the Christian Religion* (Philadelphia, PA: Westminster).

8. Charles Péguy, "Victor-Marie, Comte Hugo," *Oeuvres en Prose, 1909-1914* (Paris: Gillimarde, 1961).

Chapter 4

1. From "Choruses from 'The Rock'" in *Collected Poems 1909-1962* by T.S. Eliot; Copyright 1936 by Harcourt Brace Jovanovich, Inc.; copyright © 1963, 1964 by T.S. Eliot. Reprinted by permission of the publisher.

2. C.G. Jung, *Memories, Dreams, Reflections*, recorded and edited by Aniela Jaffe, translated by Richard and Clara

Winston (New York: Pantheon Books, a Division of Random House, Inc., copyright © 1961). Reprinted with permission of the publisher.

3. See Robert K. Greenleaf, *The Leader As Servant* (Cambridge, MA: Center for Applied Studies).

4. Dane Archer, "The Male Change of Life." Reprinted with permission from the March 1968 issue of the Yale Alumni Magazine; copyright by Yale Alumni Publications, Inc. (Further description of symptoms and problems may be found in an unpublished paper by H.C. Klemme, M.D., "Crisis of the Later Years," The Menninger Foundations, 1972)

5. See Martin Symonds, "How to Cope With Those Middle-Aged Blues," *The Reader's Digest*, November 1971.

6. K.E. Eble, *Career Development of the Effective College Teacher* (Washington, D.C.: A.A.U.P., 1971), p. 55.

7. Allen Wheelis, *The Quest for Identity* (New York: W.W. Norton, 1958), p. 207.

8. Peter Loewenberg, "Love and Hate in the Academy," *The Center Magazine*, September/October 1972, p. 8. Used by permission of the author.

9. Martin Buber, "Distance and Relation," *Psychiatry*, vol. 20, 1957, p. 102.

10. L.H. Farber, *The Ways of the Will* (New York: Harper Colophone, 1968), p. 173.

11. Peter Loewenberg, "Love and Hate in the Academy," *The Center Magazine*, op. cit., p. 11.

Chapter 5

1. See Wayne Oates, *Confessions of a Workaholic*, (Nashville TN: Abingdon, 1973).

2. George Benson, a St. Louis psychiatrist, has poignantly determined in *Then Joy Breaks Through* (New York: Seabury, 1972), the innumerable vacillations of a young woman who is suffering from depression over the course of extended therapy.

3. Katsuju Kawamata, "Balancing the Work/Life-Style Equation in Japan," *Northwest Orient Airlines Passages*, October 1974.

4. Ibid.

Chapter 6

1. From "Little Gidding" in *Four Quartets* by T.S. Eliot, copyright 1943 by T.S. Eliot; renewed 1971 by Esme Valerie Eliot. Reprinted by permission of Harcourt Brace Jovanovich, Inc.

Chapter 7

1. Galway Kinnell, "Saint Francis and the Sow," *Mortal Acts, Mortal Words* (Boston: Houghton Mifflin, 1980).
2. See Erich Fromm, *Man for Himself* (New York: Holt, Rinehart & Winston, 1947).
3. Erich Fromm, *The Revolution of Hope* (New York: Harper & Row, 1968), p. 10.
4. George MacDonald, *The Princess and Curdie* (New York: Macmillan, 1954).
5. Madeleine L'Engle, *A Circle of Quiet* (New York: Farrar, Straus & Giroux, 1972), p. 110.
6. *The New Yorker*, February 10, 1975.
7. A.J. Heschel, *The Insecurity of Freedom* (New York: Schocken, 1972), p. 82.

Chapter 8

1. Florida Scot-Maxwell, *The Measure of My Days* (New York: Knopf, 1973), pp. 73ff.

Chapter 9

1. Those interested in exploring this matter further will find a useful discussion in L. H. Farber, The Ways of the Will (New York: Harper Colophon, 1968).
2. Anne Morrow Lindbergh, "The Journey Not the Arrival," *Smith Alumnae Quarterly*, August 1978.